CURRENT TRENDS AND ISSUES IN HISPANIC LINGUISTICS

SUMMER INSTITUTE OF LINGUISTICS

PUBLICATIONS IN LINGUISTICS

Publication Number 80

EDITORS

Virgil Poulter
University of Texas
Arlington

Desmond C. Derbyshire
Summer Institute Of
Linguistics

ASSISTANT EDITORS

Alan C. Wares

Iris M. Wares

CONSULTING EDITORS

Doris A. Bartholomew
Pamela M. Bendor-Samuel
Robert A. Dooley
Jerold A. Edmondson
Austin Hale

Robert E. Longacre
Eugene E. Loos
William R. Merrifield
Kenneth L. Pike
Viola G. Waterhouse

CURRENT TRENDS AND ISSUES IN HISPANIC LINGUISTICS

LENARD STUDERUS
EDITOR

A Publication of
THE SUMMER INSTITUTE OF LINGUISTICS
and
THE UNIVERSITY OF TEXAS AT ARLINGTON
1987

© 1987 by the Summer Institute of Linguistics, Inc.
Library of Congress Catalog No: 87-062884
ISBN: 0-88312-012-7

All Rights Reserved

No part of this publication may be reproduced, stored in a retrieval system, or transmitted in any form or by any means— electronic, mechanical, photocopy, recording or otherwise— without the express permission of the Summer Institute of Linguistics, with the exception of brief excerpts in magazine articles and/or reviews.

Copies of this and other publications of the Summer Institute of Linguistics may be obtained from

> Bookstore
> Summer Institute of Linguistics
> 7500 W. Camp Wisdom Rd.
> Dallas, TX 75236

CONTENTS

Foreword vii

1. Recent Trends in Hispanic Linguistics 1
   Frank Nuessel

2. African Influence on Hispanic Dialects 33
   John Lipski

3. The Spanish Teacher as Dialectologist 69
   Mark G. Goldin

4. Noun Gender Categories in Spanish and French:
   Form-Based Analyses and Comparisons 81
   Richard V. Teschner

Foreword

The papers in this volume stem from the spring 1986 Linguistics Forum Series held at the University of Texas at Arlington and the Summer Institute of Linguistics of the International Linguistics Center in Dallas, Texas. The lectures were sponsored jointly by the Department of Foreign Languages and Linguistics of UT: Arlington and the SIL. The topic of the series, "Hispanic Linguistics," allowed us to sample some of the diverse studies recently carried out by investigators with varying interests in the Spanish language. The four researchers included here—Nuessel, Lipski, Goldin and Teschner—represent divergent yet partially overlapping interests.

The order of presentation in this volume represents the sequence of lectures as given. We begin with Nuessel's careful historical overview of recent research in Hispanic linguistics. Next is Lipski's wide-ranging analysis of the question of possible African influence in Spanish. Goldin continues the thread of dialectology as he succinctly shows its potential relevance to the teaching of Spanish. Lastly, Teschner treats Spanish within a wider Romance context as he concludes a string of research revolving around noun gender patterns in Spanish vs. French.

Both the kinds of research commented on by Nuessel and the kinds presented here by Lipski, Goldin, and Teschner offer a window into what contemporary researchers in Hispanic linguistics have been engaged in. In recent years studies like the one Nuessel presents here have become more and more valuable. This is because over the past three decades both the number of Hispanists engaged in research and publishing and the number involved in linguistic studies have increased dramatically. On top of this, the number of new linguistic models developed since the sixties, and the boom in linguistic research in general have created an acute need for better articulation among linguists of all fashions.

In the studies of Lipski, Goldin, and Teschner we find evidence in each case of both a research continuum and an historical perspective. For example, although Lipski treats an issue which relates to current research on such diverse areas as coastal Colombia and Equatorial Guinea, he also relates all this to certain Golden Age Peninsular data. Likewise, while Goldin aims to satisfy a particular need of contemporary Spanish teachers, he finds it useful to discuss at least one linguistic model which was born in the nineteenth century. And of course, Teschner takes on an issue which had begun to tantalize grammarians well over a century ago. But each of these three studies with roots in the distant past can also be seen to interlock at some point with the relatively recent field of sociolinguistics. This is of course clearest in the case of Lipski's research, which relates to pidgins, creoles, and ethnicity in general. Meanwhile, Goldin's discussion of language variation touches upon the concept of creoles as well as variation by the different sexes. And, alas, in modern-day Spanish, marking for gender has become intricately complicated by societal changes. Thus, Teschner's study completes the picture.

Lenard Studerus
University of Texas at Arlington

Recent Trends in Hispanic Linguistics
Frank Nuessel
University of Louisville

1. Introduction

In this paper, I would like to accomplish several goals. First, I wish to present an overview of recent trends and issues in Hispanic linguistics. Any such effort at first seems to be elusive, if not impossible. Therefore, I have sought to delimit this pursuit by establishing some possibly arbitrary benchmarks for expository purposes. I have chosen to limit my sources for this survey to the realm of available published treatises from journals, dissertations, conference proceedings, especially those of the annual Linguistic Symposia on Romance Languages, various *Festschriften* and related analyzable collections, etc. It is likely that even in this wide-ranging review of the literature some omissions will occur. Though inevitable, they are not intentional. In order to further restrict this summary I shall limit myself selectively to materials that have appeared in large part since the 1970s, primarily but not exclusively in North America. The two broad domains of phonology and morphology, and syntax and semantics will constitute the major focal points of this overview. Within each of the two major subdivisions, I shall focus on theories, diachronic studies, sociolinguistic analyses, applied linguistics, and other noteworthy aspects. In each of the two major headings, I shall consider a wide variety of analyses. Moreover, I shall speculate about the future in terms of what should be done and what is likely to be done.

2. Phonology and Morphology

2.1 Theoretical Studies.

As Jürgen Klausenburger (1981:197) has observed, "the decade of the '70s in phonology began with an established paradigm [cf. Kuhn 1970], the transformational generative (TGP) approach contained in Chomsky and Halle's monumental *Sound Pattern of English* (SPE) (1968)." This M.I.T.-based approach contained several fundamental principles which would be challenged in the 1970s: (1) abstract underlying forms (indicated by significant differences between phonetic and phonemic representations, absolute neutralization, the use of nonphonetic features, and the incorporation of boundary markers [cf. Cressey 1978b:87]; (2) substitution of articulatory for acoustic features; and (3) formalization of the properties of phonological rules (variables, rule interaction, boundary markers, sequenced derivations, etc.). Such a theoretical model soon failed because many young scholars discovered that this approach could not accommodate some fundamental problems. Consequently numerous innovations and variant approaches began to surface. The first serious contender to SPE was Natural Generative Phonology (NGP) as espoused by Hooper (1976) and others. This theoretical hypothesis offered several alternatives to TGP as specified by Klausenburger (1981:198): (1) concrete underlying forms (i.e., in the case of surface alternations one must be basic); (2) no extrinsic ordering conditions (i.e., rules apply whenever the structural description is met, in an intrinsic fashion, and (3) the differentiation of phonological rules which are phonetically motivated and exceptionless and morphological rules morpho-syntactically motivated.

One of the major preoccupations of NGP was the attempt to formalize the notion of syllable. Despite its desirability, Ladefoged (1982:219–24) has documented the futility of the enterprise thus far. Success in defining this concept has eluded many generations of linguists. Nevertheless, Hooper's (1972:536) informal statement about this apparently elusory entity (cf. Núñez-Cedeño 1980:36) is reproduced here as (1):

(1)
$$\emptyset \rightarrow \$ / [+\text{syll}] \left\{ \begin{array}{l} \underline{\quad} [-\text{syll}]_0^1 \quad\quad\quad\quad\quad\quad\quad\quad\quad (a) \\ [-\text{syll}]_0 \underline{\quad} \left\{ \begin{array}{l} [-\text{son}] \begin{bmatrix} +\text{son} \\ -\text{nas} \end{bmatrix}_0 \\ [+\text{cons}] [-\text{cons}]_0 \end{array} \right\} \begin{array}{l} [+\text{syll}] \quad (b) \\ \\ \quad\quad\quad\quad (c) \end{array} \end{array} \right.$$

In addition, Hooper's (1972:527) syllable insertion rule (cf. Núñez-Cedeño 1980:37) reproduced here as (2) is yet a further illustration of this reemerging interest in phonotactics ($ = syllable).

(2) a. insert a $-boundary between two contiguous syllabic segments.

  b. If there is only one nonsyllabic segment between two syllabic segments the $-boundary occurs before the nonsyllabic segment:

u$na 'one', o$so 'bear', ha$ya 'let there be', pe$ro 'but'.

c. when there are two or more nonsyllabic segments, if one is an obstruent other than /s/ and the following segment is a liquid, the syllable boundary occurs before the obstruent:

pa$dre 'father', si$glo 'century', res$plandor 'splendor'.

d. If the second nonsyllabic segment is a glide, the $-boundary occurs before the first segment:

a$byerto 'open', a$bwelo 'grandfather'.

e. otherwise, the $-boundary occurs between the two nonsyllabic segments:

is$la 'island', per$la 'pearl', al$to 'high', an$cho 'wide', es$to 'this'.

Hooper's (1976) assertions about the formal properties of the syllable were soon subjected to criticism from various linguists. In essence, Hooper's universal syllabification rule ((1) above) is a segmental insertion rule which introduces an abstract boundary marker ($) between contiguous phonological segments despite the fact that it is labeled a definition. Vennemann (1972:16) claims that "syllabification rules are persistent rules . . . i.e., anywhere rules: After each step in a derivation, the string is checked against the syllabification rules, and resyllabification occurs if there is a conflict." Núñez-Cedeño (1980:43) states that resyllabification is a blatant extrinsic ordering ploy (cf. Koutsoudas, Sanders, and Noll 1974). This same linguist ultimately grants amnesty to this definition by stating that it belongs to the metatheory and consequently is not a part of the rule component. I shall return to the syllable briefly after a few remarks concerning the directions of phonological theory in the late seventies and early eighties.

The explosion of new theories, which was a reaction to SPE, was most obvious at the Indiana University at Bloomington Conference on the Differentiation of Current Phonological Theories (September 30–October 1, 1977) and subsequently published as Dinnsen (1979). This convergence of approximately 400 linguists proved to be a showcase for numerous divergent approaches of phonological theory.

Autosegmental phonology has become one of several new theoretical approaches to Hispanic phonology in the eighties (the others are lexical phonology and metrical phonology). It should be noted, at this juncture, that no single theory has come to dominate theoretical phonology in the manner in which the SPE model did in the sixties and seventies (cf. Hayes 1986:467). In his important essay in Dinnsen (1979), Goldsmith describes autosegmental phonology (originally an attempt to deal with the so-called prosodic or suprasegmental aspects of language such as stress, tone, intonation, etc.) as a "multi-linear phonological analysis in which different features may be placed on separate tiers, and in which the various tiers are organized by 'association lines' and a Well-Formedness Condition; and . . . analysis of phonological phenomena less in terms of feature-changing rules as such and more in terms of rules that delete and *reorganize* the various autosegments through the readjustment of the association lines" (1979:202).

A significant result of Goldsmith's work is the elimination of one of the major class features [syllabic]. Goldsmith states that "the feature *syllabic* is redundant and many if not all of the traditional rules adjusting the value of the feature *syllabic* or inserting glides homorganic with neighboring vowels . . . should rather be dealt with in terms of autosegmental notions of adjustment of association lines at the syllabic level" (1979:222, note 5). In fact, Selkirk (1984b:107) has even argued for the elimination from phonological theory of all the major class features ([syllabic], [consonantal], and [vocalic]).

It is worth noting a few aspects of autosegmental phonology (cf. Goldsmith 1976, Holt 1984). First, it differs from conventional SPE generative phonology in that this approach views phonological units as tiered components which permit subsegmental units within a segment rather than having isolated and essentially indivisible elements. These multidimensional autosegments have connectors, or association lines which permit the phonologist to account for the overlapping properties of such phenomena as tonal contours, etc. This subsegmental or stratified view of phonology offers a mechanism for explaining the overlapping acoustic perceptions of certain linear phonetic processes such as nasalization (cf. Clayton 1985).

A seminal autosegmental study is Goldsmith (1981, originally presented in 1979 at the Ninth Linguistic Symposium on Romance Languages) in which that linguist broke ground on the apparently noncontroversial area of point-of-articulation assimilation rules (cf. Cressey 1974) in Spanish. In the same essay Goldsmith also treated briefly the issue of aspiration (cf. Goldsmith 1979) and spirantization (cf. Lozano 1978, Danesi 1982, other comments below).

While autosegmental phonology is one of the newer theories applied to Spanish, other approaches are equally important. Lexical phonology (Mohanan 1982), for example, is another theory that has been applied to Spanish data on occasion. Harris (1984:78) specifies some of the basic properties of this theory:

(3) a. Any rule that has lexical exceptions applies in the lexicon (though not every rule has exceptions).

   b. Rules sensitive to the internal structure of words are lexical rules.

   c. Lexical rule applications are cyclic.

In addition, Harris states that lexical phonology "makes the following claims about phonological representations in the lexicon" (1984:78):

(4) a. Predictable values of features are not specified in underlying representations of lexical items.

   b. Unspecified feature values are filled in by language-particular rules and universal markedness rules.

   c. Language-particular rules apply before universal rules.

Both Harris (1984), and Guitart (1985) have applied lexical phonology to Spanish data in order to deal with certain classic phonological processes in Spanish, namely nasal assimilation (Harris 1984), aspiration, nasal velarization, and liquid gliding (Guitart 1985).

Harris, whose influential recent book (1983), deals with the application of metrical phonological theory to Spanish data, is a prime mover in this new wave of innovative reanalysis of old problems in Hispanic phonology and morphology that have seemingly defied previous resolution or invite reconsideration in a new framework. Several linguists have espoused variations of this theoretical approach (Halle and Vergnaud 1980, Hayes 1981, Liberman 1978, McCarthy 1982, Selkirk 1984a). These different versions of metrical hypotheses have enriched phonological theory by allowing a fuller concept of the prosodic component through the implementation of additional theoretical apparatus such as the introduction of layered autonomous tiers, namely a vocalic tier, a consonantal tier, and syllabic skeleton (McCarthy 1982). In fact, the title of one important work in this domain is "Three-dimensional phonology" (Halle and Vergnaud 1980). The implementation of a metrical grid (Liberman 1978:198–206, Selkirk 1984a) is yet another formal proposal. Núñez-Cedeño (1985b) provides an excellent introduction to a version of metrical theory with an application to Spanish data.

In many regards, the reanalyses of traditional and unresolved problems in Hispanic phonology have marked the virtual renaissance of this domain of linguistic theory as applied to Spanish. During much of the mid-to-late seventies, studies of Spanish phonology seemed moribund as manifested in the paucity of investigations in this domain in comparison to investigations of syntax and semantics which had been receiving far greater attention in terms of published research.

In 1978, I noted (Nuessel 1978:208) that the primary areas of attention in Hispanic phonology were: (1) diphthongization, (2) stress assignment, (3) plural formation, (4) lexical stratification, and (5) glide formation. In the eighties, all except lexical stratification have received reinterpretations within new theoretical frameworks. A brief excursus on these reappraisals of earlier studies is worth mentioning at this point. Each reference will specify the theoretical framework employed by an author.

2.1.1. Diphthongization. The phenomenon of diphthongization has always proven resistant to systematic analysis because the only way to differentiate diphthongizing from nondiphthongizing vowels is to use an ad hoc nonphonetic feature [D(diphthongizing)] (cf. Harris 1969:116–18). Shuldberg (1984) has looked at these same data in a metrical framework and has, unfortunately, not resolved this enigmatic problem. This author reintroduces the arbitrary feature [+D] in order to contend with these perplexing verbal forms. Shuldberg justifies this position by stating that such a nonphonetic feature carries a meaning of its own. That signification is precisely that these items continue to circumvent unitary explanation. Recapitulation of the history of Castilian seems to be the only theoretical resolution. The question arises, of course, about the psychological reality of such an approach (cf. Skousen 1975:8) which presupposes that children have encoded in their brains a sophisticated knowledge of the diachrony of Spanish. Amastae (1982) examines related data from nonstandard dialectical variations in an SPE framework.

2.1.2. Stress Assignment. The second area in which reinterpretation of the SPE analytical model has received renewed attention is stress assignment. It is appropriate that this suprasegmental aspect be reconsidered given the fact that the prosodic structure of languages was one of the prime reasons for the development of nonlinear phonological theories. In this regard, Harris (1983) and Núñez-Cedeño (1985a) have examined the stress system in light of metrical phonology. Harris (1983) proposes a metrical analysis of stress assignment for nonverbs, while Núñez-Cedeño (1985a) argues for a unified metrical statement for the assignment of stress in the verbal system which he ultimately extends to all categories. The metrical approach resolves old problems through the use of the phonological cycle but has recourse to fairly abstract underlying forms. In its favor is the fact that this proposal eliminates the need for parenthetical notation and the special diacritic features of earlier segmental analyses (Harris 1969, 1975; Hooper and Terrell 1976) and provides an integrated explanation for all categories.

2.1.3. Plural Formation. Plural formation is the third territory that has provided the grist of many an article and which has as its fundamental point the abstract/concrete debate. Harris (1970) argued for an apocope approach to this segment of the phonology/morphology interface. Saltarelli (1970, 1972), on the other hand, proffered an epenthetic solution. I have called this a pseudo-issue but I must acknowledge Lipski's (1974:85) insightful observation that "the pluralization process has the methodological attraction of being less complex than the often nightmarishly irregular verb paradigms, but still variegated enough to provide a suitable setting for the suspenseful tracking down of elusive generalizations which provides the spice for modern theoretical linguistics."

Harris (1980a), based on Contreras' (1977) devastating proof that an apocope abstract approach to pluralization is wrong, has now adopted a concrete or epenthetic resolution to this problem. His nonconcatenative autosegmental reanalysis of the problem seems to have resolved the outstanding polemic, at least for the moment. This particular case, at least, shows that contemporary linguistic theory is amenable to modification and is not an inflexible monolithic entity.

2.1.4. Glide Formation. Finally, glide formation has been subjected to more recent reinspection by various linguists. Harris (1969) and Cressey (1975) concur in their belief that there exist underlying glides and vowels which are subsequently transformed into glides. Later, Cressey (1978a) rejected this position. Harris (1980b) points to a possible resolution of the glide problem through a metrical analysis. Holt (1984) finally provided an autosegmental account of this phenomenon which requires two rules of glide formation ordered before and after stress assignment. This is, of course, a return to a position originally rejected by Harris (1969:31). In this case, at least, one finds an autosegmental analysis less than illuminating; or at best, no worse than the earlier analysis. Most recently, Morgan (1984) has argued for a unitary source for front and back glides which integrates several theoretical viewpoints (Mohanan 1982, Clements and Keyser 1983).

In addition to the aforementioned theoretical reconsiderations of earlier concatenative analyses (diphthongization, stress assignment, plural formation, and glide formation), several additional stimulating innovations have taken place in the realm of spirantization, aspiration, and point of articulation rules.

The proper description of voiced consonants /b, d, g/ has been reconsidered. Conventional wisdom (Harris 1969:38-40) claims that such segments derive from underlying stops. More recently, Lozano (1978), Goldsmith (1979), Danesi (1982), and Mascaró (1984) have made different claims. Lozano, for example, believes that such segmental phonemes derive from an "underspecified" archisegment which generates both continuants and noncontinuants from one source. Danesi (1982) argues persuasively for a similar solution on the basis of several theoretical considerations: (1) a stop ⇒ continuant rule is an "elsewhere rule"; and (2) articulatory phonetic considerations. In addition to these points, there are statistical, dialectical, and historical considerations that militate in favor of this new approach.

Aspiration rules (s ⇒ h) have been reinterpreted in an autosegmental scheme. Goldsmith (1979:6) has shown that this procedure captures the fact that such changes involve the deletion of the oral autosegment yet retain the laryngeal gesture of voicelessness.

Point of articulation rules (e.g., nasal assimilation) have received much attention. Cressey (1974) deserves credit for his pioneer work on what amounts to a quasi-autosegmental version of point of articulation rules when he grouped such phenomena together under the cover symbol PA (point of articulation). I must note that I had been somewhat unflattering in my original annotation (Nuessel 1978:215) of this seminal and visionary article. Harris (1984) has also reexamined one such rule (nasal assimilation) in an autosegmental and lexical phonological framework.

In the past, excesses in theoretical phonology have occurred in which erroneous or even outrageous hypotheses have been generated through misguided zeal. Therefore, firmly grounded empirical analyses based on replicable experiments may serve to combat theoretical intemperance. Examples of studies that accomplish this include Torreblanca (1984) and Williams (1982).

2.2 Diachronic Studies

Several handbooks of varying degrees of detail are now available. Lapesa's (1981) venerable and exhaustive overview of the history of the language has had its bibliographic references updated, thus rendering it much more useful. Next, Resnick's (1981) recent book with its fine exemplification and careful explanation of basic theoretical concepts serves as a useful primer. Finally Burt (1980) is the least sophisticated, and consequently, the least useful of this trio.

Besides the three overviews just mentioned, several individual studies reflect some of the areas of historical investigation. Hartman (1984, 1985), for example, has done pioneer work in disproving some commonly held myths about sound changes. In addition to this helpful endeavor, this same linguist, at times in collaboration with Carlos Otero, has carried out groundbreaking work in the development of phonological rules on a computer program to simulate actual diachronic events. This ongoing project will do much to enhance the pedagogical and scholarly efforts in this field. In the area of etymological studies, Menocal (1984) has likewise debunked some prevailing fictions about certain lexical items of Arabic provenience. In addition, no one can ignore the voluminous contributions of Yakov Malkiel, whose recent retirement in 1985 in no way diminishes that Romance philologist's lifelong scholarly activity and productivity in the realm of Hispanic as well as Romance linguistics. Any attempt at enumerating this individual's prodigious contributions would require more time and space than this presentation permits, though a forthcoming special issue of *Romance Philology* will contain a comprehensive bibliography.

Another noteworthy study that has appeared is Alvar and Pottier's (1983) historical morphology of Spanish. Virtually atheoretical, this monumental book is a two-decade collaborative effort of two of Europe's finest Romance philologists. Extensive analysis of diachronic derivational and inflectional morphology is the core of their work. This labor of love leaves no stone unturned in its attempt to document all attested forms of divergent morphemes.

Fleischman (1982) has examined the history of the Spanish future tense in her volume on Romance. This linguist has restated the traditional outcome of that tense in Castilian, i.e., synthesis⇒analysis⇒synthesis; this reflects Givón's (1971:126) dictum that "morphology recapitulates syntax." Fleischman, however, has analyzed some new data provided by Anderson (1979) which shows a new future tense formation that results from the agglutination of the periphrastic form with the verb *ir* (e.g., *yo vadormir*). This fascinating data set has led Fleischman to speculate that Spanish may be entering into a new synthetic phase of the Romance syntactic cycle.

2.3. Sociolinguistic Studies

Sociolinguistics, defined here as "the study of the characteristics of language varieties, the characteristics of their functions and the characteristics of their speakers as these three constantly interact, change, and change one another within a speech community" (Fishman 1972:4), is an area in which phonetic variation has continued to receive increasing attention. This subdomain of linguistics has a wide variety of approaches from linguistic variation, languages in contact, diglossia, the ethnography of communication, etc. (cf. Amastae and Elías-Olivares 1982).

In another domain, Lipski (1983, 1985b) has examined the public or official uses of Spanish on the airwaves and concludes that there is a striking homogeneity (1983:239) of pronunciation or radio speech (1985b:228) despite the heterogeneous backgrounds of announcers. This fact has implications for the professional training of radio broadcasters and also militates against the claim that a regional dialect is necessary for success in the field.

Several authors have examined the current status and possible outcomes of so-called syllable-final or "weak" consonants, especially word or syllable-final *-s* (cf. Hooper 1976:208; Núñez-Cedeño 1980). In this regard, Uber (1984) believes that this sound (and *-n*) in the speech of Puerto Rican Spanish speakers will continue to "weaken." Among the numerous other studies on final *-s* are those by Lipski (1985a) who provides a synchronic perspective on the phenomenon in Central America while illuminating its historical development. López Scott (1983) has studied the process in a Honduran dialect and has shown that aspiration of /s/ is now spreading to initial position of word and syllable —long considered to be a strong position— hence far less subject to modification. Likewise, Hundley (1983) has studied the outcomes of V + /s/ in Peruvian Spanish. In general, most dialect studies are now being carried out in the framework of Labovian sociolinguistics (Labov 1969). In this regard, Lope Blanch (1976), however, has penned a most informative essay on the similarities and differences between sociolinguistics and dialectology, as well as their relatedness. One exception to this trend is Reyes' (1978) description of Chicano Spanish which blends SPE theory and dialectology into a truly harmonious blend. Reyes' study is the finest description of vocalic modification in fast speech ever to appear. For a relatively recent overview of dialectology, López Morales (1976) offers a good perspective.

2.4 Applied Linguistics

In this domain, several noteworthy occurrences may be reported. Computer-assisted instruction represents one of the realms in which an explosive amount of activity is being recorded. The fact that *Hispania* now has a separate rubric ("Computers in Research and Teaching") for this facet of the profession testifies to its impact. Moreover, *The Modern Language Journal* has a subdivision in its review section labeled "Software." Underwood (1984), in his prize-winning (Kenneth W. Mildenberger Award) book *Linguistics, computers, and the language teacher,* has documented the utility of carefully prepared and selected computer software in both the instructional and language acquisition tasks.

Kvavik (1976, 1981) has done some groundbreaking analysis in the difficult domain of intonation. She has observed (1976:406), correctly, I believe, that this area "is one of the least understood areas of Spanish phonology. There has been a paucity of research, and the void is reflected in the quality and scope of current pedagogical applications. Recent analytical developments in the field suggest that a reexamination of the linkage between basic research and pedagogical applications is in order, for established ideas have been challenged." This position echoes the views of both Dalbor (1980:208) and Resnick (1975). Because of a relative scarcity of theoretical agreement, a lack of a unified descriptive formalism, and the time-consuming nature of such studies, few scholars have delved into this domain. For this reason, Kvavik deserves credit from her peers for her virtual career-long dedication to this formidable, yet crucially important aspect of linguistic investigation. Lantolf (1976b) has also authored a significant essay in this same area.

In addition, Barrutia and Terrell (1982) have coauthored a new textbook on phonetics. This opus has received mixed reviews and is unlikely to supplant Dalbor's (1980) now classic work on the same subject.

Hispania has come to recognize the need to apply linguistic analysis to the various instructional levels. This is evident in that publication's new departmentalization, though a recent editorial by Theodore Sackett (1985:808) bemoaned the lack of manuscripts in its new "Pedagogy" section.

2.5. Morphological Studies

This subheading is probably misleading because it divorces morphology from phonology even though both are intimately linked. I have chosen to use this rubric as a place to situate certain innovative analyses directed at the Romance languages in general but including Spanish examples as a data set.

Piera (1984), for example, addresses the thorny question of portmanteau words (such as *conmigo*) which are unanalyzable into a linear level of discrete components and the alternation of *el/la* followed by a feminine noun beginning with stressed *a.* Plank (1984:341) ultimately proposes a universal adjacency constraint in such cases. Nevertheless, this restriction is segmental in nature.

In addition to the theoretically based morphological studies just alluded to, Teschner and Muñoz (1984) have done a statistical analysis on the irregularities in the verb system which have theoretical, pedagogical and cognitive implications. Likewise, Teschner and Russell (1984) have examined the gender patterns of Spanish nouns. This also has potential pedagogical applications. In the same vein, Harris (1985:35) has studied so-called word markers, or rightmost elements of a noun, which are described as having "no grammatical properties at all, aside from their phonological shape and distribution: they are simply small pieces of phonological material that must be at the right place at the right time" (1985:35).

Finally, Jaeggli (1980) has written possibly one of the best systematic treatises on one type of Spanish diminutive ever to have appeared in print. In this essay, carried out in an autosegmental framework, Jaeggli describes the introduction of *-it-* and *-ecit-* as an infixation process.

Bybee, whose contributions in the area of Natural Generative Phonology (Hooper 1972, 1976) are significant, is currently engaging in groundbreaking morphological research that deserves mention. In her essay in Dinnsen's volume (Hooper 1979), an important new focus on morphology may be found. In that conference paper, Bybee first began to explore some of the distinctive properties of morphology including "an almost disconcerting tolerance of exceptions, irregularities and competing generalizations" (Hooper 1979:113).

Bybee has continued to pursue the complex domain of morphology in an effort to clarify some of its many puzzles. In many of her studies, she has utilized Spanish data as a point of departure because it possesses relatively intricate morphological patterns. Bybee (1980), for example, examined various factors in morphophonemic change in order to sustain her claim that such change is the result of "synchronic generalizations that speakers construct" (1980:45). In order to support the claims made in that study, Bybee and Pardo (1981) devised a nonce-probe experiment with nonexistent verbs in order to see how native speakers would treat these forms. This innovative foray into experimental morphology not only yielded interesting results that substantiate her hypotheses, but such an approach sets the stage for additional experimental verification of sometimes controversial theoretical assertions. Bybee's most recent work is a book (Bybee 1985) which is a culmination of and unification of her earlier theoretical investigations into morphology. This monograph is likely to be as important as her earlier volume on Natural Generative Phonology (Hooper 1976).

2.6 Summary

This portion of this report makes it clear that much work is taking place in a variety of domains in Hispanic phonology and morphology. Innovations are evident everywhere. They would include the following points:

(5) a. Application of novel theories (autosegmental phonology, metrical phonology, and lexical phonology) to existing data including dialect material which was formerly a descriptive enterprise only. This represents the reassertion of the domination of M.I.T.-based linguistics on linguistic theory and application in general. While this trend has resurrected the somewhat languid area of phonology and morphology, one must question the virtual domination of a domain of linguistics by approaches from a single source.

b. Succession of sociolinguistic analysis (the use of language in context) over formerly descriptive dialect studies (cf. Lope Blanch 1976).

c. Continuation of interest in diachronic studies.

d. Improvement in the quality of applied linguistic studies.

e. Investigation of the interface of phonology, morphology, and syntax.

3. Syntax and Semantics

3.1. Theoretical Studies

In March 15, 1979, the Conference on Current Approaches to Syntax was held at the University of Wisconsin at Milwaukee and was designed to parallel the Phonology symposium held in Bloomington, Indiana a year and a half earlier. At that major linguistic event, at least thirteen distinct theories were presented and compared with other competitors (cf. Moravcsik and Wirth 1980). These included: (1) cognitive grammar. (2) corepresentational grammar, (3) daughter-dependency grammar, (4) epiphenomenal grammar, (5) equational grammar, (6) functional grammar, (7) functionally interpreted base-generated grammar, (8) Montague grammar, (9) relational grammar, (10) role and reference grammar, (11) stratificational grammar, (12) tagmemics, and (13) trace theory. Of these thirteen grammatical hypotheses, only three have been applied to Spanish data. Even fewer have been consistently employed by linguists for Hispanic grammar. Tagmemics, for example, has been used sparingly (Brend 1968). Relational grammar has enjoyed more application. Finally, trace theory, in a sense the forerunner of Chomsky's government and binding theory (Chomsky 1980, 1981), has seen a far wider range of usage in the eighties.

In that same year (Nuessel 1979b), I surveyed those linguistic theories that had been applied to Spanish. At that time, I concluded that only three major approaches had been applied in any systematic way to various fragments of Spanish grammar. Those theoretical models were: (1) the Standard Theory as outlined in Chomsky's *Aspects of the theory of syntax* (1965); (2) Generative Semantics as espoused by many of Chomsky's brightest former students including George Lakoff, James D. McCawley, John Robert Ross, and Paul Postal, and (3) Case Grammar as set forth by Charles J. Fillmore (1968), and Walter A. Cook (1978) among others. The standard theory was applied to various grammatical constructions in many a doctoral dissertation during the past two decades. Likewise, generative semantics, which was to be a short-lived theory (cf. Newmeyer 1980), also saw its share of applications. Goldin (1968) and McCoy (1969) were the most notable examples of the application of case grammar to Spanish.

In that essay (Nuessel 1979b), I also examined six areas of syntax to which these three theories had been applied. They were: (1) pronominalization, (2) sentential complementation, (3) relativization, (4) mood selection, (5) negation, and (6) verbal categorization. All but item (6) have received more intense scrutiny by linguists in the last decade. In this overview, I would like to examine those same areas in order to specify what has been done since 1979 (cf. Nuessel 1979a, 1981) and indicate the most recent trends.

3.1.1. Pronominalization. Clitic pronouns in general, and *se* constructions in particular, have generated the largest number of studies in this realm. Lantolf (1976a:191) has observed with regard to the latter that there are usually two approaches to the analysis of *se* structures, namely, "utilize data provided by *se* constructions to advance linguistic theory ... or implement previously developed linguistic theory to explain *se* constructions as language specific phenomena." Of course, this observation is relevant to all theories applied to Spanish and to all Spanish grammatical constructions. These structures have probably received so much attention because they seem to be semantically anomalous. These forms are nonparadigmatic (Suñer 1973), i.e., they occur only in the third person. Likewise, impersonal *se* constructions do not admit a reflexive interpretation. Thus, this relatively unique grammatical construct acquires a secondary significance or meaning which is often rendered as a passive in English. In many ways, the cognitive processing of this complex grammatical structure may even parallel strategies employed for decoding metaphors (cf. the studies contained in Miall 1982 for critiques and explications of such theories). More will be said about these complex constructions later.

In the seventies, clitics were receiving a great deal of attention in terms of their surface order (cf. Perlmutter 1971), i.e., surface filters or constraints on their positioning as well as their origin, i.e., either base generation (cf. Strozer 1976) or transformational derivation (cf. Smith 1975).

In the past decade, Zwicky (1977) and Carstairs (1981) have tried to define the basic properties of clitic forms. In this regard, Carstairs (1981:4) provides a helpful summary of the basic properties of both clitics and inflectional affixes which he labels with the neutral term *appendages:*

(6) a. Appendages are BOUND forms (that is, they cannot occur as independent sentences).

b. There are tight restrictions on the position of appendages relative to either (a) (roots or stems belonging to) particular parts of speech or (b) adjacent constituents of surface structure.

c. They are more or less phonologically parasitic, tending to combine with neighboring phonologically defined "words" in matters such as stress placement or vowel harmony.

d. They often have an anaphoric function, "echoing" elements elsewhere in the sentence.

e. Their shape is often affected by grammatical features (e.g., number, gender, conjugation-type, or declension-type) of the item which governs their position . . . If we call this item the ANCHOR of the appendage, we can summarize this characteristic by saying appendages are often sensitive to their anchors.

f. They are often members of a relatively small closed system, one of whose members must always appear at the relevant place in the structure.

These forms attract linguists because they are bridges between the conventional linguistic modules (not to be confused with the Government-Binding notion of modules, cf. van Riemsdijk and Williams 1986:223–311) of phonology, morphology, syntax, semantics and the lexicon. In many ways, these forms are difficult to situate in an appropriate linguistic module. First, clitics display features that are morphophonological in that their placement affects syllabic structure, stress assignment, and other phonetic features of the language. In fact, their mere existence wreaks havoc with a proper definition of the notion "word." Second, these same elements have syntactic properties such as stringent requirements on their placement, ordering, and movement. Finally, their meaning obeys certain principles of reference or "binding" to a proper antecedent.

One possible fruitful avenue of research in the realm of clitics involves the consideration of cofactors such as mood selection as a means of determining clitic promotion. Luján (1980) has done the most extensive study of this kind. Suñer (1980), likewise, has isolated three semantic categories of predicates which license clitic climbing. In the latter, it should be noted that such movement is not strictly syntactic but obeys incompletely understood semantic constraints.

3.1.2. Sentential Complementation. Early analyses of the noun clause and its derivative forms dealt almost exclusively with theoretical models of structure. In the past decade, much of the active research has centered upon causative constructions. These limited and problematic substructures are of great interest because of their syntactic compression. These constructs manifest themselves as infinitives often in association with clitic pronouns (see above). These structures, consequently, are semantically amorphous and hence open to multiple interpretations because they may have an active or passive meaning, and clitic pronouns may be subjects or objects. The latter is the result of extremely complex and incompletely understood rules of movement for such pronominal forms (cf. Luján 1980, Suñer 1980). Most of the current work is extremely theoretical in nature and Spanish is simply a testing ground for theory validation or clarification. Zagona (1981), for example, is one of a growing number of linguists struggling to find satisfactory explanations for these complex constructions. Burzio (1983) has examined causatives in two Romance languages (Italian and French) and some of his analytical discoveries are potentially applicable to Spanish. The Romance causative (Italian, French, and Spanish data) is the subject of a recent article by Zubizarreta (1985). She attributes five basic properties to such constructions (pp. 247–52):

(7) a. Lexical structure specifies the number of arguments that a verb takes and the semantic role(s) (Agent, Theme, Goal, Location, etc.) that each argument bears.

  b. [P]redicates make a distinction between two types of arguments in their lexical structure; namely between the external and the internal arguments. The external argument is syntactically identified as the one that is realized in the [NP, S] position in a clause. The internal arguments are syntactically realized inside the VP (i.e., sisters of the verb).

  c. Besides the semantic value of its arguments, a verb specifies the syntactic frame within which the internal arguments are realized.

  d. The semantic role of an argument that is realized as a prepositional phrase is restricted by the preposition.

  e. [L]exical structure specifies referential indices.

Finally, Finneman (1982) is the most comprehensive account of this grammatical configuration currently available. This author defines a causative in the following terms (p. 8):

(8) a. Let A and B be predicates.

    b. A causative relationship exists between two predicates, A and B if:

      1. A entails B

      2. Not-A entails not-B, all else equal.

    c. A is an effect predicate.

    d. The construction involving A and B is then a causative construction.

Not only is this dissertation a fine study of a particular syntactic element, but it also ranks as one of the best works in the field in recent years.

3.1.3. Relativization. This is an area in which a great deal of linguistic endeavor has been occurring. Until Chomsky's various treatises on WH-movement and government and binding theory (1977, 1980, 1981), this feature of Spanish grammar received scant attention with the exception of Cressey's (1966) early inspection of these constructs in an *Aspects* (Chomsky 1965) framework.

Within the past half dozen years, several meticulous treatises have been published on relativized structures. Rivero (1978, 1980a, 1980b, 1981, 1984) has researched the multiple and labyrinthine properties of this structure more than any other linguist. Noteworthy contributions have also come from Plann (1980), Contreras (1984), and D'Introno (1984) to name but a few.

3.1.4. Mood Selection. The plethora of studies on mood determination has been well documented by Bell (1980). The continuing interest in this topic attests to the fact that no one has ever provided a comprehensive analysis of this phenomenon. Because a proper determination of the factors involved in mood choice is so elusive, new generations of linguists will continue to probe its mysteries. In reality, mood is predictable in most cases and hence not problematic. The difficulty lies in that small group of cases in which mood choice is optional. In these instances, the factors that lead to that selection appear to be impenetrable. This, then, is the arena for theory modification and destruction.

One notable recent study in this domain includes Castronovo's (1984) remarkable overview of studies in the field since the last century. On the other hand Solano-Araya's (1982) resolution of the issue of mood choice is desirable but too simplistic. The complexities surrounding just one facet of mood selection, namely, past temporal reference, may be found in Studerus' (1981) article on this topic which alludes to Dalbor's (1969) eye-opening article on the same theme.

3.1.5. Negation

In this realm, Bosque (1980) provides an in-depth analysis of one aspect of negation in Spanish — negative polarity items. These are defined (1980:26) as "all those grammatical units that can produce the syntactic effects of the adverbial *no* by facilitating the appearance of a N[egative] P[olarity] I[tem]. These elements elicit or induce the same syntactic mechanisms as explicit negation without their necessarily acquiring its syntactic properties" [translation mine FN]. Not included in his book are the following important related areas: (1) affixal negation; (2) colloquial negative expressions; (3) multiple negation in complex sentences; (4) positive polarity items; (5) the behavior of negatives in syntactic constructions unrelated to polarity, and (6) the scope of negation. Gyurko (1971) and Zimmer (1964) have already studied (1) in some detail. Likewise, Ibáñez (1972) has treated item (2) at length. Negation remains one of the least understood areas of linguistic analysis and, in this regard, Spanish is no exception.

3.2. New Areas of Study

3.2.1. Agreement Phenomena. The study of what may be called occurrences of disagreement in Spanish have been steadily increasing. These include violations of subject-verb concord and noun-adjective agreement. One of the reasons for this newfound interest in such data is the fact these constructions appear to be agrammatical (cf. Otero 1972, 1973, 1975), i.e., they are technically incapable of being generated according to certain conventional rule formulations. Yet, despite this anomalous situation, grammars continue to produce them. Moreover, such constructions, though unlicensed by the grammar, reflect semantic or cognitive perceptions about certain structures that may constitute a window into the way language is processed and learned.

The classic study is Otero's (1972:237) often-cited case of impersonal *se* reproduced here.

(9) a. *Se alquila* (singular) *los apartamentos.*

   b. *Se alquilan* (plural) *los apartamentos.*

This classic example has focused on the competency/performance distinction (Chomsky 1965:4). Westphal would claim that the b sentence above is a case of optional verb-direct object agreement (cf. Aissen 1973). More recently, in fact, this issue and the wider problem of subject-verb concord has been the locus of study related to reformulation and improvement of government and binding theory (Chomsky 1981). Specifically, this theoretical approach has attempted to establish explicit procedures for linking NPs to the appropriate verbal ending. Much needs to be resolved, but this avenue of investigation seems promising.

Other related studies include Schroten (1981), Suñer (1982a), and Nuessel (1984) on subject-verb disagreement and Wonder (1985) on adjective-noun discordance. This field has by no means been exhausted. Suñer (1982b) also examines cases of subjectless predicates such as *haber* in which that verb may undergo optional object agreement.

3.2.2. Personal a. The recent attention given to the "personal *a*" construction has done little to illuminate its resistance to uniform explanation. The three most recent essays (King 1984; Kliffer 1984; Weissenreider 1985) refute earlier analysis and struggle to explain this grammatical structure. Weissenreider (1985), at least, dismisses the two prevailing principles concerning this form, namely, the Ambiguity Principle which states that this particle distinguishes subject and object in those sentences where this verbal relation is ambiguous. Likewise, this same author denies the validity of the Lexical Principle which states that certain verbs have an *a* associated with them as a part of their meaning. Weissenreider's solution is a vague Principle of Semantic Distance which is never set forth as a discrete statement.

3.2.3. Ser and Estar. This set of problematic predicates will, in all likelihood, continue to be the source of innumerable articles and treatises because of the difficulty encountered by nonnative speakers in the differentiation of the usage of these two verbs. In their hierarchy of difficulty, Stockwell, Bowen, and Martin (1965:285) speak of the negative correspondence in the native language (English) and the difficulties of split choices in which "English has a rule or category which corresponds with a pair of Spanish ones that are obligatorily distinguished." Copular *ser* and *estar* are excellent examples of this phenomenon.

Recently, a pair of scholars has been examining these two verbs within a modified Case Grammar framework. Franco and Steinmetz (1983, 1985) and Franco (1984) have studied the uses of these two verbs with locatives and with qualifying adjectives. Because of the dichotomous nature of these predicates, such a theoretical approach is likely to be the most fruitful and productive pedagogical perspective. In an interesting comparative analysis (with Catalan), Falk (1979) analyzed this pair of verbs used with attributive adjectives. Many more essays are available but those just listed represent some of the recent accounts on the topic. Luján (1981) relates the aspectual features "perfective/imperfective" with these two predicates as a means of distinguishing their appropriate usage. This insightful analysis correlates *estar* predicates with a clearly delimited time and *ser* predicates with an undelimited time frame. This aspectual dichotomy captures succinctly the traditional distinction of essential vs. accidental.

3.3. Sociolinguistic Studies

The trend toward sociolinguistic studies of syntax has been relatively recent. Most of the efforts in this subdiscipline concern variation of verbal forms based on contextual or socially determined factors. One area that has been studied by various authors is the *-ra/-se* distinction of the past subjunctive. Whalen (1979) has examined this as a synchronic phenomenon in Spanish while Wilson (1983) considers the diachronic dimensions of these verbal forms. Silva-Corvalán (1984a) offers a very interesting perspective of such forms based on a population sample in Covarrubias, Spain.

Silva-Corvalán has also done some very interesting work on temporal and aspectual variation (cf. Dahl 1985) in spoken Spanish (Silva Corvalán 1983, 1984b).

Another notable sociolinguistic work is Woolford's (1983) application of generative grammatical theory to bilingual code-switching (cf. Grosjean 1982).

3.4. Applied Studies

In general, applied linguistics means linguistic analysis applied to the teaching of Spanish to nonnative (often English) speakers. Many of the articles published in *Hispania* have this as a basic focus. Thus, Terrell and Salgués de Cargill's (1979) opus is directly related to such efforts. This work is significant because it provides instructors in this field with a useful and up-to-date text written in Spanish.

The area of pragmatics is another realm which lays some claim to being an applied area, in that speech act theory specifies how language is used in real life. The ability to specify these details has major implications for foreign language pedagogy as well as related social scientific disciplines. Studerus (1974, 1975) has done groundbreaking work in this field. Haverkate (1979, 1984) has likewise excelled in the description of discourse analysis in Spanish. Such important factors as referential strategies, lexical choice, selection of certain syntactic constructions, and rules of conversation all contribute to communication in important yet subtle ways.

More recently, the whole issue of language problems and language planning as related to Spanish is beginning to be seriously addressed. In a sense, this is a case of sociolinguistics applied to the resolution of particular socially significant linguistic problems. In an excellent anthology of articles by respected linguists (Elías-Olivares et al. 1985), the multiple dimensions of this sociolinguistic aspect have been considered in terms of description and use. In one of the chapters of this anthology, Rubin (1985) points out the many domains that must be considered in language planning: health and medicine, law, employment, communication, citizenship and representation, social welfare and education, to name but a few of the realms that language touches.

3.5. Summary

The second portion of this overview demonstrates that much research is occurring in the realm of syntax and semantics. The following points seem clear:

(10) a. The reassertion of the dominance of M.I.T-based theory is obvious (cf. Newmeyer 1980). In this realm, topics like relative clause structures and agreement phenomena are receiving far greater attention than in the past. Likewise, the increase in research related to causatives is opening new horizons of study.

b. New inroads are being made in the application of various sociolinguistic theories to certain syntactic variables. Such studies provide clues as to how social forces affect language use.

c. Applied studies are increasing in dimension and scope. No longer is such work purely pedagogical. Rather, these efforts are being directed at new areas of study.

d. The integration of analysis is another emerging aspect of the field. Works such as those of Luján (1980) and Suñer (1980) are beginning to examine so-called cofactors in linguistics, i.e., associated phenomena which may be linked in an indirect fashion.

4. Conclusion

This abbreviated review of some of the most significant highlights of current research in Hispanic linguistics leads to at least one major conclusion. Ours is an active field, populated by many dedicated theoreticians and practitioners who are endeavoring to enlighten all aspects of the mysteries of the Spanish language. Despite the fact that there exist several unified reference bases for activity in the field on an annual basis (*The MLA International Bibliography, The Year's Work in Modern Language Studies, Bibliographie linguistique, The Comparative Romance Linguistics Newsletter*, etc.), little integration of vast amounts of work that occurs every year takes place. These central clearinghouses of information seem not to promote an integration of the vast storehouse of knowledge already created. The fragmentary approach to the study of the Spanish language continues.

This grapeshot approach to Hispanic linguistics is troublesome, especially in light of the fact that the most recent research points to the interface of the traditional linguistic modules of phonology, morphology, syntax, semantics, and the lexicon (cf. Selkirk 1984a).

REFERENCES

Aissen, Judith. 1973. "Shifty objects in Spanish." *Papers from the ninth regional meeting, Chicago linguistic society,* ed. by Claudia Corum et al. pp.11–22. Chicago: Chicago Linguistic Society.

Alvar, Manuel and Bernard Pottier. 1983. *Morfología histórica del español.* Biblioteca Románica Hispánica III. Manuales, 57. Madrid: Editorial Gredos.

Amastae, Jon. 1982. "Mid vowel raising and its consequences in Spanish." *Linguistics* 20:175–202.

Amastae, Jon, and Lucía Elías-Olivares eds. 1982. *Spanish in the United States: sociolinguistic aspects.* Cambridge, England: Cambridge University Press.

Anderson, Eric. 1979. "The development of the Romance future tense: morphologization II and a tendency toward analyticity." *Papers in Romance* 1:21–35.

Barrutia, Richard, and Tracy David Terrell. 1982. *Fonética y fonología españolas.* New York: Wiley.

Bell, Anthony. 1980. Mood in Spanish: a discussion of some recent proposals. Hispania 63:377–90.

Bosque, Ignacio. 1980. *Sobre la negación.* Madrid: Ediciones Cátedra, S. A.

Brend, Ruth. 1968. *A tagmemic analysis of Mexican Spanish clauses.* The Hague: Mouton.

Burt, John R. 1980. *From phonology to philology: an outline of descriptive and historical linguistics.* Washington, D.C.: University Press of America.

Burzio, Luigi. 1983. Conditions on representation in Romance. *Linguistic Inquiry* 14:193–222.

Bybee, Joan L. 1980. Morphophonemic change from inside and outside the paradigm. *Lingua* 50:45–59

———. 1985. *Morphology: a study of the relation between meaning and form.* Amsterdam/Philadelphia: John Benjamins.

——— and Elly Pardo. 1981. "On lexical and morphological conditioning of alternations: a nonce-probe experiment with Spanish verbs." *Linguistics* 19:937–68.

Carstairs, Andrew. 1981. *Notes on affixes, clitics and paradigms.* Bloomington, IN: Indiana University Linguistics Club.

Castronovo, Brian Joseph. 1984. "A critical analysis of interpretations of the Spanish subjunctive from Bello to the present." Ph.D. dissertation, University of Wisconsin, Madison. [D.A.I. 1985. 45:2086-A.]

Chomsky, Noam. 1965. *Aspects of the theory of syntax.* Cambridge, MA: MIT Press.

———. 1977. "On *wh* movement." *Formal syntax,* ed. by P. Culicover, T. Wasow, and A. Akmajian, pp. 71–133. New York: Academic Press.

———. 1980. "On binding." *Linguistic Inquiry.* 11:1–46.

———. 1981. *Lectures on government and binding.* Dordrecht: Foris.

Chomsky, Noam, and Morris Halle. 1968. *The sound pattern of English.* New York: Harper & Row.

Clayton, Mary L. 1985. "Trying to make the data stand still: continuity, gradience and indeterminacy in Spanish phonology." *Current issues in Hispanic phonology and morphology,* ed. by Frank Nuessel, pp. 1–13. Bloomington. IN: Indiana University Linguistics Club.

Clements, George and Samuel Keyser. 1983. *CV phonology: a generative theory of the syllable.* Cambridge, MA: MIT Press.

Contreras, Heles. 1977. "Epenthesis and stress assignment in Spanish." *University of Washington Working Papers in Linguistics* 3:9–33.

———. 1984. "Multiple questions in English and Spanish." *Papers from the XIIth linguistic symposium on Romance languages,* ed. by Philip Baldi, pp. 121–33. Amsterdam: Benjamins.

Cook, Walter. 1978. *Case grammar: development of the matrix model* (1970–1978). Washington, D.C.: Georgetown University Press.

Cressey, William W. 1966. "A transformational analysis of the relative clause in urban Mexican Spanish." Ph.D. dissertation. University of Illinois, Urbana-Champaign. [D.A.I. 1967. 27:3857-A.]

———. 1974. "Homorganic in generative phonology." *Papers in Linguistics* 7:69–81.

———. 1975. "Spanish glides revisited." *1974 colloquium on Spanish and Portuguese linguistics,* ed. by W. G. Milán, John J. Staczek, and Juan C. Zamora. pp. 35–43. Washington, D.C.: Georgetown University Press.

———.1978a. "Absolute neutralization of the phonemic glide-versus-vowel contrast in Spanish." *Contemporary studies in Romance linguistics,* ed. by

Margarita Suñer, pp. 90–105. Washington, D.C.: Georgetown University Press.

——— .1978b. *Spanish phonology and morphology: a generative view.* Washington, D.C.: Georgetown University Press.

Dahl, Östen, 1985. *Tense and aspect systems.* Oxford: Blackwell.

Dalbor, John B. 1969. Temporal distinctions in the Spanish subjunctive. *Hispania* 52:889–96.

——— . 1980. *Spanish pronunciation: theory and practice.* 2nd ed. New York: Holt, Rinehart and Winston.

Danesi, Marcel. 1982. "The description of Spanish /b, d, g/ revisited." *Hispania* 65:252–58.

Dinnsen, Daniel A. 1979. *Current approaches to phonological theory.* Bloomington: Indiana University Press.

D'Introno, Francesco. 1984. "Relativization." *Papers from the XIIth linguistic symposium on Romance languages,* ed. by Philip Baldi, pp. 135–52. Amsterdam: Benjamins.

Elías-Olivares, Lucía, et al., editors. 1985. *Spanish language use and public life in the USA.* Berlin: Mouton.

Falk, Johan. 1979. *Ser y estar con atributos adjetivales. Anotaciones sobre el empleo de la cópula en catalán y en castellano.* I. Acta Universalis Uppsaliensis: Studia: Studia Romanica Uppsaliensis, XXIX. Uppsala.

Fillmore, Charles J. 1968. "The case for case." *Universals in linguistic theory,* ed. by Emmon Bach and Robert T. Harms, pp. 1–88. New York: Holt, Rinehart and Winston.

Finneman, Michael David. 1982. "Aspects of Spanish causative constructions." Ph.D. dissertation. University of Minnesota. [D.A.I. 1983. 43:1131-A.]

Fishman, Joshua A. 1972. *Sociolinguistics: A brief introduction.* Rowley, MA: Newbury House.

Fleischman, Suzanne. 1982. *The future in thought and language: diachronic evidence from Romance.* Cambridge: Cambridge University Press.

Franco, Fabiola. 1984. "'Ser' y 'estar' + locativos en español." *Hispania* 67:74–79.

——— . 1985. "A deeper look at the grammar and some implications of SER and ESTAR + locative in Spanish." *Hispania* 68:641–48.

———— and Donald Steinmetz. 1983. "Ser y estar + adjetivo calificativo en español." *Hispania* 66:176–84.

Givón, Talmy. 1971. "Historical syntax and synchronic morphology." *Papers from the seventh regional meeting, Chicago Linguistic Society*, pp. 394–415. Chicago: Chicago Linguistic Society.

Goldin, Mark G. n. d. [1968]. *Spanish case and function*. Washington, D.C. Georgetown University Press.

Goldsmith, John. 1976. *Autosegmental phonology*. Bloomington, IN: Indiana University Linguistics Club.

————. 1979. "The aims of autosegmental phonology." *Current approaches to phonological theory*, ed. by Daniel A. Dinnsen, pp. 202–22. Bloomington: Indiana University.

————. 1981. "Subsegmentals in Spanish phonology: an autosegmental approach." *Linguistic symposium on Romance languages 9*, ed. by William W. Cressey and Donna Jo Napoli, pp. 1–16. Washington, D.C.: Georgetown University Press.

Grosjean, François. 1982. *Life with two languages: an introduction to bilingualism*. Cambridge, MA: Harvard University Press.

Guitart, Jorge M. 1985. "Variable rules in Caribbean Spanish and the organization of phonology." *Current issues in Hispanic phonology and morphology*, ed. by Frank Nuessel, pp. 28–33. Bloomington, IN: Indiana University Linguistics Club.

Gyurko, L. A. 1971. "Affixal negation in Spanish." *Romance Philology*. 20:225–40.

Halle, Morris and Jean-Roger Vergnaud. 1980. "Three dimensional phonology." *Journal of Linguistic Research* 1:83–105.

Harris, James W. 1969. *Spanish phonology*. Cambridge, MA: MIT Press.

————. 1970. "A note on Spanish plural formation." *Language* 46:928–30.

————. 1975. "Stress assignment rules in Spanish." *Colloquium on Spanish and Portuguese linguistics*, ed. by William G. Milán, John J. Staczek, and Juan Zamora, pp. 56–83. Washington, D.C.: Georgetown University Press.

————. 1980a. "Nonconcatenative morphology and Spanish plurals." *Journal of Linguistic Research* 1:15–31.

————. 1980b. "Palatal -Ø alternations in Spanish." *Contemporary studies in Romance languages*, ed. by Frank Nuessel, pp. 108–30. Bloomington, IN: Indiana University Linguistics Club.

———. 1983. *Syllable structure and stress in Spanish: a nonlinear analysis.* Linguistic Inquiry Monograph 8. Cambridge, MA: MIT Press.

———. 1984. Autosegmental phonology, lexical phonology, and Spanish. *Language sound structure*, ed. by Mark Aronoff and Richard T. Oehrle, 67–82. Cambridge, MA: MIT Press.

———. 1985. Spanish word markers. *Current issues in Hispanic phonology and morphology*, ed. by Frank Nuessel. pp. 34–54. Bloomington, IN: Indiana University Linguistics Club.

Hartman, Steven Lee. 1984. "On the history of Spanish *macho*." *Hispanic Linguistics* 1:97–114.

———. 1985. "On opening black boxes: Latin -*nge*- and -*ng'l*- in Hispano-Romance." *Selected papers from the XIIIth linguistic symposium on Romance languages*, ed. by Larry D. King and Catherine A. Maley, 149–62. Amsterdam: John Benjamins.

Haverkate, Henk. 1979. *Impositive sentences in Spanish.* Amsterdam: North-Holland.

———. 1984. *Speech acts, speakers, and hearers: reference and referential strategies in Spanish.* Amsterdam: Benjamins.

Hayes, Bruce. 1981. *A metrical theory of stress rules.* Bloomington, IN: Indiana University Linguistics Club.

———. 1986. "Assimilation as spreading in Toba Batak." *Linguistic Inquiry* 17:467–99.

Holt, Katherine Drexel. 1984. "An autosegmental approach to syllabification in Spanish." *Papers from the XIIth linguistic symposium on Romance languages*, ed. by Philip Baldi, pp. 169–93. Amsterdam: Benjamins.

Hooper, Joan B. and Tracy Terrell. 1976. "Stress assignment in Spanish." *Glossa* 10:64–110.

Hooper, Joan B. 1972. "The syllable in phonological theory." *Language* 48:525–40.

———. 1976. *An introduction to natural generative phonology.* New York: Academic Press.

———. 1979. "Substantive principles in natural generative phonology." *Current approaches to phonological theory*, ed. by Daniel Dinnsen, 106–25. Bloomington: Indiana University Press.

Hundley, James Edward. 1983. "Linguistic variation in Peruvian Spanish: unstressed vowel and /s/." Ph.D. dissertation, University of Minnesota. [D.A.I. 1983. 44:743–A.]

Ibáñez, R. 1972. *Negation im Spanischen.* Munich: Fink.

Jaeggli, Osvaldo. 1980. "Spanish diminutives." *Contemporary studies in Romance languages,* ed. by Frank Nuessel, pp. 142–58. Bloomington, IN: Indiana University Linguistics Club.

King, Larry D. 1984. "The semantics of direct object A in Spanish language & linguistics." *Hispania* 67:397–403.

Klausenburger, Jürgen. 1981. "Romance phonological studies in the '70s." *Proceedings of the tenth anniversary symposium on Romance linguistics,* ed. by Heles Contreras and Jürgen Klausenburger. Seattle. WA: University of Washington. *Papers in Romance* (Supplement II), 3:197–213.

Kliffer, Michael D. 1984. "Personal 'a,' kinesis and individuation." *Papers from the XIIth linguistic symposium on Romance languages,* ed. by Philip Baldi, pp. 195–216. Amsterdam: Benjamins.

Koutsoudas, Andreas, Gerald Sanders, and Craig Noll. 1974. "On the application of phonological rules." *Language* 50:1–28.

Kuhn, Thomas S. 1970. *The structure of scientific revolutions.* Chicago: University of Chicago Press.

Kvavik, Karen H. 1976. "Research and pedagogical materials on Spanish intonation: a reexamination." *Hispania* 59:406–17.

———.1981. "Spanish multiaccent intonations and discourse functions." *Current research in Romance languages,* ed. by James P. Lantolf and Gregory B. Stone, pp. 46–62. Bloomington, IN: Indiana University Linguistics Club.

Labov, William. 1969. "Contraction, deletion and inherent variability of the English copula." *Language* 45:715–62.

Ladefoged, Peter. 1982. *A course in phonetics.* 2nd ed. New York: Harcourt Brace Jovanovich.

Lantolf, James P. 1976a. Review of *Concerning the deep structures of Spanish reflexive sentences* by Jan Schroten. The Hague: Mouton. *General Linguistics* 16:191–206.

———. 1976b. "On teaching intonation." *The Modern Language Journal* 60:267–74.

Lapesa, Rafael. 1981. *Historia de la lengua española.* Madrid: Gredos.

Lavandera, Beatriz R. 1984. *Variación y significado.* Buenos Aires, Argentina: Librería Hachette.

Liberman, Mark Y. 1978. *The intonational system of English*. Bloomington, IN: Indiana University Linguistics Club.

Lipski, John M. 1974. "Toward a production model of Spanish morphology: a further look at plurals." *Studia Linguistica* 28:83–99.

———. 1983. "La norma culta y la norma radiofónica: /s/ y /n/ en español. *Language Problems and Language Planning* 7:239–62.

———. 1985a. "/s/ in Central American Spanish." *Hispania* 68:143–49.

———. 1985b. "Spanish in United States Broadcasting." *Spanish language use and public life in the USA*, ed. by Lucía Elías-Olivares, Elizabeth A. Leone, René Cisneros, and John Gutiérrez, pp. 217–33. Berlin: Mouton.

Lope Blanch. Juan M. 1976. "La sociolingüística y la dialectología hispánica." *1975 Colloquium on Hispanic linguistics*, ed. by Frances M. Aid, Melvyn C. Resnick, and Bohdan Saciuk, pp. 67–90. Washington, D.C.: Georgetown University Press.

López Morales, Humberto. 1976. "Nuevas tendencias en la dialectología del caribe hispánico." *1975 Colloquium on Hispanic linguistics*, ed. by Frances M. Aid, Melvyn C. Resnick, and Bohdan Saciuk, pp. 91–108. Washington, D.C.: Georgetown University Press.

López Scott, Alma Leticia. 1983. "A sociolinguistic analysis of /s/ variation in Honduran Spanish." Ph.D. dissertation, University of Minnesota. [D.A.I. 1983. 44:2752-A.]

Lozano, María del Carmen. 1978. *Stop and fricative alternations: fortition and spirantization processes in Spanish phonology*. Bloomington, IN: Indiana University Linguistics Club.

Luján, Marta. 1980. "Clitic promotion and mood in Spanish verbal complements." *Linguistics* 18.381–484.

———. 1981. "The Spanish copulas as aspectual indicators." *Lingua* 54:165–210.

McCarthy, John M. 1982. *Formal problems in Semitic phonology and morphology*. Bloomington, IN: Indiana University Linguistics Club.

McCoy, A. M. C. B. 1969. "A case grammar classification of Spanish verbs." Ph.D. dissertation, University of Michigan. [D.A.I. 1971. 31:3534-A.]

Mascaró, Joan. 1984. "Continuant spreading in Basque, Catalan, and Spanish." *Language sound structure*, ed. by Mark Aronoff and Richard T. Oehrle, pp. 287–98. Cambridge, MA: MIT Press.

Menocal, María Rosa. 1984. "The mysteries of the orient: special problems in Romance etymology." *Papers from the XIIth linguistic symposium on Romance languages,* ed. by Philip Baldi, pp. 501-15. Amsterdam: Benjamins.

Miall, David S. 1982. *Metaphor: problems and perspectives.* Atlantic Highlands, NJ: Humanities Press.

Mohanan, K. P. 1982. *Lexical phonology.* Bloomington, IN: Indiana University Linguistics Club.

Moravcsik, Edith A. and Jessica R. Wirth. 1980. *Syntax and semantics.* Volume 13, Current approaches to syntax. New York: Academic Press.

Morgan, Terrell A. 1984. "Consonant-glide vowel alternations in Spanish: A case study in syllabic phonology." Ph.D. dissertation, University of Texas at Austin. [D.A.I. 1985. 46:966-A.]

Newmeyer, Frederick. 1980. *Linguistic theory in America.* New York: Academic Press.

Nuessel, Frank. 1978. "An annotated, critical bibliography of generative-based grammatical analyses of Spanish: phonology and morphology." *The Bilingual Review* 5:207-37.

———. 1979a. An annotated, critical bibliography of generative-based grammatical analyses of Spanish: syntax and semantics. *The Bilingual Review* 6:39-80.

———. 1979b. "An overview of syntactic theories applied to Spanish: 1968-1979." *Lektos* 1:109-26 (new series).

———. 1981. "Tendencias actuales y temas de discusión en sintaxis española." *Estudios filológicos* 16:175-82.

———. 1984. "(Dis)agreement in Spanish." *Papers in Linguistics* 17:267-81.

Núñez-Cedeño, Rafael A. 1980. *La fonología moderna y el español de Santo Domingo.* Colección Ensayo No. 2. Santo Domingo: Taller.

———. 1985a. "Stress assignment in Spanish verb forms." *Current issues in Hispanic phonology and morphology,* ed. by Frank Nuessel, pp. 55-76. Bloomington, IN: Indiana University Linguistics Club.

———. 1985b. "On the three-tiered syllabic theory and its implications for Spanish." *Selected papers from the XIIIth linguistic symposium on Romance languages,* ed. by Larry D. King and Catherine A. Maley, pp. 261-85. Amsterdam: Benjamins.

Otero, Carlos. 1972. "Acceptable ungrammatical sentences in Spanish." *Linguistic Inquiry* 3:233-42.

———. 1973. "Agrammaticality in performance." *Linguistic Inquiry* 4:551–62.

———. 1975. "On acceptable agrammaticality: a rejoinder." *Linguistic Inquiry* 7:342–61.

Perlmutter, David M. 1971. *Deep and surface structure constraints in syntax.* New York: Holt, Rinehart, and Winston.

Piera, Carlos. 1985. "On the representation of higher order complex words." *Selected papers from the XIIIth linguistic symposium on Romance languages*, ed. by Larry D. King and Catherine A. Maley, pp. 287–313. Amsterdam: Benjamins.

Plank, Frans. 1984. "Romance disagreements: phonology interfering with syntax." *Journal of Linguistics* 20:329–49.

Plann, Susan. 1980. *Relative clauses in Spanish without overt antecedents and related constructions.* Berkeley: University of California Press.

Resnick, Melvyn C. 1975. *Phonological variants and dialect identification in Latin American Spanish.* The Hague: Mouton.

———. 1981. *Introducción a la historia de la lengua española.* Washington, D.C.: Georgetown University Press.

Reyes, Rogelio. 1978. *Studies in Chicano Spanish.* Bloomington, IN: Indiana University Linguistics Club.

Riemsdijk, Henk van, and Edwin Williams. 1986a. *Introduction to the theory of grammar.* Current Studies in Linguistics 12. Cambridge, MA: M.I.T. Press.

Rivero, María-Luisa. 1978. "Topicalization and *wh* movement in Spanish." *Linguistic Inquiry* 9:513–17.

———. 1980a. "On left dislocation and topicalization in Spanish." *Linguistic Inquiry* 11:363–93.

———. 1980b. "Theoretical implications of left-branch modifiers in Spanish." *Linguistic Analysis* 6:407–61.

———. 1981. "WH-movement in comparatives in Spanish." *Linguistic symposium on Romance languages 9*, ed. by William W. Cressey and Donna Jo Napoli, pp. 177–96. Washington, D. C. Georgetown University Press.

———. 1984. "Diachronic syntax and learnability: free relatives in thirteenth century Spanish." *Journal of Linguistics* 20:81–129.

Rubin, Joan. 1985. "Spanish language planning in the United States." *Spanish language use and public life in the USA*, ed. by Lucía Elías-Olivares, et al., pp.133–52. Berlin: Mouton.

Sackett, Theodore. 1985. "Hispania in its new format: problems and opportunities." *Hispania* 68:808.

Saltarelli, Mario. 1970. "Spanish plural formation: apocope or epenthesis." *Language* 46:89–96.

———. 1972. "Epenthesis, velar softening and stress in Spanish." *Linguistische Berichte* 19:63–68.

Saporta, Sol and Heles Contreras. 1962. *A phonological grammar of Spanish*. Washington: University of Washington Press.

Schroten, Jan. 1981. "Subject deletion or subject formation: evidence from Spanish." *Linguistic Analysis* 7:121–69.

Selkirk, Elisabeth O. 1984a. *Phonology and syntax: the relation between sound and structure*. Cambridge: MIT Press.

———. 1984b. "On the major class features and syllable theory." *Language sound structure*, ed. by Mark Aronoff and Richard T. Oehrle, pp. 107–36. Cambridge, MA: MIT Press.

Shuldberg, Howard Kelly. 1984. "Diphthongization in Spanish verbs." *Hispanic Linguistics* 1:215–27.

Silva-Corvalán, Carmen. 1983. "Tense and aspect in oral Spanish narrative." *Language* 59:760–80.

———. 1984a. "The social profile of a syntactic-semantic variable: three verb forms in old Castile." *Hispania* 67:594–601.

———. 1984b. "A speech event analysis of tense and aspect in Spanish." *Papers from the XIIth linguistic symposium on Romance languages*, ed. by Philip Baldi, pp. 229–51. Amsterdam: Benjamins.

Skousen, Royal. 1975. *Substantive evidence in phonology*. The Hague: Mouton.

Smith, Rosslyn Hall (Mynatt). 1975. "Spanish clitic pronouns: a transformational description." Ph.D. dissertation, University of New Mexico. [D.A.I. 1975. 36:3640-A-3641-A.]

Solano-Araya, Miguel. 1982. "Modality in Spanish: an account of mood." Ph.D. dissertation. University of Kansas. [D.A.I. 1983 43:3898-A.]

Stockwell, Robert P. J., Donald Bowen, and John W. Martin. 1965. *The grammatical structures of English and Spanish*. Chicago: University of Chicago Press.

Strozer, Judith. 1976. "Clitics in Spanish." Ph.D. dissertation, University of California, Los Angeles. [D.A.I. 1977. 37:6541-A.]

Studerus, Lenard H. 1974. "Imperativity as a universal: Spanish paraphrases." Ph.D. dissertation. University of Colorado. [D.A.I. 1974. 35:2302-A.]

———. 1975. "Spanish imperatives and the notion of imperativity." *Hispania* 58:518–23.

———. 1981. "A Spanish twilight zone: mood, syntax, and past temporal reference." *Hispania* 64:97–103.

Suñer, Margarita. 1973. "Non-paradigmatic *se*'s in Spanish." Ph.D. dissertation, Indiana University, Bloomington. [D.A.I. 1973. 34:1882-A.]

———. 1980. "Clitic promotion in Spanish revisited." *Contemporary studies in Romance languages*, ed. by Frank Nuessel, pp. 300–30. Bloomington, IN: Indiana University Linguistics Club.

———. 1982a. "On null subjects." *Linguistic Analysis* 9:55–78.

———. 1982b. *Syntax and semantics of Spanish presentational sentence-types*. Washington, D.C.: Georgetown University Press.

Terrell, Tracy David and Maruxa Salgués de Cargill. 1979. *Lingüística aplicada a la enseñanza del español al anglohablante*. New York: Wiley.

Teschner, Richard V., and Bro. Frank Muñoz. 1984. "Statistics on morphological irregularity in Spanish verb tenses." *Hispania* 67:99–104.

——— and William M. Russell. 1984. "The gender patterns of nouns: an inverse dictionary-based analysis." *Hispanic Linguistics* 1:115–31.

Torreblanca, Máximo. 1984. "El ensordecimiento de grupos biconsonánticos sonoros en el español peninsular." *Hispanic Linguistics* 1:35–40.

Uber, Diane Ringer. 1984. "Phonological implications of the perception of -*s* and -*n* in Puerto Rican Spanish." *Papers from the XIIth linguistic symposium on Romance languages*, ed. by Philip Baldi, pp. 287–99. Amsterdam: Benjamins.

Underwood, John H. 1984. *Linguistics, computers, and the language teacher*. Rowley, MA: Newbury.

Vennemann, Theo. 1972. "On the theory of syllabic phonology." *Linguistische Berichte* 18:1–18.

Weissenreider, Maureen. 1985. "The exceptional uses of the accusative *a*." *Hispania* 68:393–98.

Westphal, Germán. 1980. *Subjects and Pseudo-subjects in Spanish: the verb agreement question in the impersonal* se *construction*. Carbondale, IL/Edmonton, Canada: Linguistic Research.

Whalen. Gillian Hamer. 1979. "A study of the imperfect subjunctive variants in Spanish." Ph.D. dissertation, Cornell University. [D.A.I. 1979. 40:3275-A-3276-A.]

Williams, Stephanie Angela. 1982. "An acoustic analysis of the Spanish sound system." (Volumes I and II). Ph.D. dissertation, Georgetown University. [D.A.I. 1983. 43:2986-A.]

Wilson, Joseph Michael. 1983. "The *-ra* and *-se* forms in Mexico: a diachronic examination from non-literary sources." Ph.D. dissertation, University of Massachusetts. [D.A.I. 1984. 44:3054-A.]

Wonder, John P. 1985. "Género natural, género gramatical." *Hispania* 68:273–83.

Woolford, Ellen. 1983. "Bilingual code-switching and syntactic theory." *Linguistic Inquiry* 14:520–36.

Zagona, Karen. 1981. "Predication and the interpretation of causative complements." *Current research in Romance languages,* ed. by James P. Lantolf and Gregory B. Stone, pp. 221–31. Bloomington, IN: Indiana University Linguistics Club.

Zimmer, Karl E. 1964. "Affixal negation in English and other languages: an investigation of restricted productivity." Supplement to *Word* 20.

Zubizarreta, María Luisa. 1985. "The relation between morphophonology and morphosyntax: the case of Romance causatives." *Linguistic Inquiry* 16:247–89.

Zwicky, Arnold M. 1977. *On clitics*. Bloomington, IN: Indiana University Linguistics Club.

African Influence on Hispanic Dialects
John Lipski
University of Houston

It is apparent to any linguist who has explored the domain of Latin American Spanish dialectology, particularly in the diachronic dimension, that the currently available theories regarding the relative contributions of Andalusian and Castilian dialects, Amerindian languages, and spontaneous independent formations are in their totality not adequate to explain both the diversity and the unity of the Spanish language as spoken across two continents. One of the most interesting and at the same time most controversial facets of Latin American dialectology is the African connection, the byproduct of hundreds of thousands of African slaves imported to the New World, who spoke a variety of African languages and sometimes also European languages. In many areas of Latin America, the African population significantly outnumbered the Europeans for some time, including regions not currently noted for African cultural remnants, such as central Mexico, highland Colombia and Bolivia, and much of Chile, Paraguay, Uruguay and Argentina. In other regions, including the Caribbean, parts of Central America and the northern Pacific coast of South America, where plantation or urban slave labor continued over several centuries, the African presence is noteworthy even today, not only in the physical characteristics of many residents but also across wide-ranging cultural domains. The African contribution to the Hispanic American lexicon is undisputed, since in addition to the hundreds of Africanisms found in the local level in dialects of Spanish throughout the Caribbean and South America, such words as *marimba, mucama, guineo, congo, ñame, cachimbola, merengue, mandinga,* and *mondongo* are more widely used. A more controversial area is the possible African contribution to Spanish American morphology, syntax and especially phonetics, with the latter possibility either overlooked or overemphasized by the principal Africanist theories of Latin American dialectology.

There is literary evidence beginning at the dawn of the Spanish Golden Age that black Africans living in Spain spoke Spanish deficiently and with peculiar deformations, not only confusing grammatical categories such as gender, number and verb conjugations, but also with certain phonetic modifications.[1] These Africans were known as *bozales*, a term referring to slaves born and raised in Africa, who spoke European languages only with great difficulty; such speech is first described for 15th century Portugal, where blacks made up nearly half the population of metropolitan Lisbon for a while,[2] and where writers like Gil Vicente and Antonio de Chiado incorporated bozal Portuguese in their literary works. Bozal Spanish makes its appearance following the beginning of the 16th century, in works by Gil Vicente, Rodrigo de Reinosa, Feliciano de Silva, Quiñones de Benavente, Lope de Vega, Lope de Rueda, Sánchez de Badajoz, Simón Aguado, Góngora and Quevedo. In Latin America, early evidence of bozal Spanish comes in works by Sor Juana Inés de la Cruz and Gabriel de Santillana, who transcribed the speech of black slaves in the Caribbean and Mexico at the beginning of the 17th century, with characteristics similar to those found in Spain (Lipski 1985c; a, b).

Some early writers offered specific, if stereotyped, descriptions of bozal modifications; Quevedo remarked, for example, that in order to speak guineo (as he called Africanized Spanish), it sufficed to interchange /l/ and /r/ whenever they occurred: thus Francisco become Flancisco, *pobre* 'poor' became *poble*, and so forth. Despite the obvious exaggeration, interchange of /l/ and /r/ did figure in the literary depiction of partially Europeanized black Africans during the 15th and 16th centuries. Other phonetic traits of early bozal Spanish include, in addition to many apparently random and idiosyncratic shifts: (a) loss of syllable- and word-final /s/: *Jesús* > *Jesú; Francisco* > *Flasico*; (b) loss of the multiple trill /r̄/ in favor of the single tap [r]: *perro* > *pero* 'dog'; (c) interchange of /y/ and /ñ/: *llamar* > *ñamar* 'to call'; (d) interchange of intervocalic /d/ and /r/: *boda* > *bora* 'wedding'; (e) interchange of syllable-final /l/ and /r/: *cuerpo* > *cuelpo* 'body'; (f) loss of word-final /r/, especially in verbal infinitives: *correr* > *coré* 'to run'; (g) appearing somewhat later, vocalization of syllable-final /l/ and /r/: *carta* > *caita* 'letter.' In considering literary documents, both early and more recent, one must exercise considerable caution, most of all because it is impossible to rule out stereotyping, exaggeration and outright fabrication of "Africanized" Spanish, since the authors in question were poets and playwrights and not phoneticians and anthropologists. This is adequately demonstrated in contemporary Latin American literature in which authors attempt to depict popular phonetic tendencies in the speech of their characters, revealing ex-

---

[1] Principal studies include Weber de Kurlat (1962), Chasca (1946), Castellano (1961), Granda (1969, 1978), Jason (1967); see also Lipski (1985c; a, b, e).

[2] Pike (1967), Sanders (1982), Vila Vilar (1977), Franco Silva (1979), Carriazo (1954).

aggerations and inaccuracies, despite several centuries of accumulated expertise in literary representations of popular speech (Lipski 1985c). Another, less easily discarded factor in the speech of sixteenth and seventeenth century black slaves in Spain and Spanish America is the possible substratum of creole Portuguese. Spain bought the majority of its slaves from Portuguese slave traders during the first two centuries of the Afro-American slave trade, and due to the nature of the Portuguese slaving empire, many of the slaves had apparently acquired a rudimentary pidgin or maritime Portuguese before being transferred to other regions. The Portuguese maintained *feitorias* or slave depots in Angola, São Tomé, Fernando Poo, Cape Verde, Annobom and later Brazil, in addition to supplying some of the market from blacks already resident in southern Portugal. We have ample and indisputable evidence of the creole or pidgin Portuguese that sprang up as a lingua franca along nearly all of western and southern Africa and much of coastal Asia; this type of speech was evidently also used by slaves who spoke different and mutually unintelligible African languages, although the claims that such populations were deliberately chosen to minimize uprisings may have been overstated.

If we examine Spanish Golden Age literary documents with an eye toward creole Portuguese, instead of simply deficient Spanish, it becomes obvious that a Portuguese element did exist in bozal Spanish; examples include the change /Cl/ > /Cr/ (*blanco* > *branco* 'white,' *esclavo* > *escravo* 'slave'), and such lexical items as *bai* 'go, to go,' *muito* 'much,' the creole Portuguese subject pronoun *amí* and the Arabic borrowing in Afro-Lusitanian lingua franca *taybo* 'good.' The importance of creole and pidgin Portuguese goes far beyond sixteenth century Lisbon and Seville, since many specialists in creole languages have postulated, based on comparative evidence, that this early Portuguese creole was the basis for most if not all European-based creoles in Africa, the Caribbean and southern and southeastern Asia. If we compare the Portuguese-derived creoles of Annobon, Cape Verde, Guinea-Bissau, and São Tomé with the Spanish- and Portuguese-based Papiamentu of the Netherlands Antilles and the lingua of the Colombian village of Palenque de San Basilio, we note structural similarities too great to be due to chance development in unrelated areas; such comparisons underlie claims that this same Portuguese-creole basis was relexified and aided in forming creole dialects of English and French in the Caribbean and Africa, Spanish and Portuguese in Asia, and Dutch in the West Indies, Guyana and possibly South Africa.[3]

Without going any farther afield, the importance of the creole Portuguese

---

[3] This has been suggested by Naro (1978), Granda (1978), Valkhoff (1966), Le Page (1977), Hancock (1975), Whinnom (1965), Megenney (1983, 1984, 1985), among others. See also Alleyne (1971), Boretzky (1983), Mintz (1971), Reinecke (1938), Bickerton (1977), De Bose (1977), Todd (1974), Meier and Muysken (1977), Allsopp (1977), Taylor (1971), Perl (1982, a).

hypothesis for Africanist theories of Spanish dialectology should be obvious, for in its most radical form, this monogenetic Portuguese creole hypothesis indicates that this speech mode underlay virtually all of the bozal groups found in Spanish America over a period of more than three centuries, and therefore was more important than the strictly African element in determining the characteristics of bozal Spanish and its possible repercussions in general Latin American Spanish. At the same time, other investigators have attempted to trace phonetic and even morphological characteristics of Latin American Spanish directly to postulated African substrata, comparing patterns in West African languages most commonly attested among slave groups with those of different Spanish dialects in order to postulate wide-scale interference modes.

Since the variation among African languages is so enormous, almost any conclusion may be drawn if the comparative nets are cast wide enough, and new avenues of approach must be broached in order to shed further light on the problem of the African influence on Spanish world-wide. In particular, hypotheses as to the possible creole Portuguese substratum in Latin American Spanish, the postulated unity or identity of bozal Spanish across wide expanses of time and space, and the direct African contributions to Latin American Spanish phonology and morphology may be further tested and refined in several parallel and complementary fashions (Lipski e). The first consists of the discovery of Hispanic creole dialects that can be demonstrated to derive from sources other than the postulated 15th and 16th century Afro-Lusitanian creole, or in which such early Portuguese elements form only a small percentage of the total structure and do not account for the essential nature of the dialects in question. The second test case for the strong monogenetic hypothesis involves studying comparable situations of Afro-Hispanic linguistic interfacing, which failed to produce creole structures of the sort found in acknowledged Afro-Lusitanian creoles. Finally, it may be possible to discover dialects in which linguistic phenomena similar or identical to those occurring in Afro-Romance creoles have resulted in situations in which the Afro-Lusitanian and direct African connection is demonstrably absent. The successful demonstration of such cases would indicate that while an Afro-Portuguese base may be a sufficient condition for the formation of many creoles, and for the characteristics of the various bozal Spanish manifestations, it is not a necessary concomitant, in that other factors may converge to produce similar or identical results. In the following remarks, I will attempt to survey recent developments in Afro-Hispanic dialectology, principally those in which I have personally participated, with an eye toward assessing the prospects for pan-Hispanic Africanist theories and for a determination of the African component of Latin American Spanish.

It was long felt that no creolized dialect of Spanish had ever existed in the New World, unlike the creolized French, English, Dutch and Portuguese which continue to be spoken. Subsequently, study of Spanish American folkloric and literary evidence turned up indications of distinctly creolized language spoken by African slaves and their descendants in such areas as Cuba, Puerto Rico, the Dominican Republic and Ecuador, some of which survived until well into the present century (Granda 1978; González and Benavides 1982, Perl 1982, a; Lipski 1985c; a, c). Only a few decades ago, studies were begun on the now famous creole dialect of Palenque de San Basilio in Colombia, which greatly resembles Papiamentu and Afro-Portuguese creoles (Escalante 1954, Bickerton and Escalante 1970, Friedemann and Patiño Roselli 1983). As a result of such findings, the perspective on Afro-Hispanic studies has been shifted partially, away from the search for direct Afro-American links to the postulate of an intermediate pan-Hispanic creole stage, which through contact with European Spanish following the abolition of slavery and the assimilation of the black population into the mainstream of Latin American society gradually came to resemble regional Latin American Spanish more and more, while perhaps transferring some of its own characteristics to the Spanish spoken by descendants of Europeans.

Let us consider first the possible African influences on Latin American Spanish phonetics. If we leave out occasional and sporadic phonetic deformations of early Africanized Spanish and consider only those consistent and persistent phenomena, we are left with: loss of syllable- and word-final /s/, interchange, loss and occasional vocalization of syllable-final /l/ and /r/, and occasional neutralization of intervocalic /d/ and /r/. To this we may add velarization of word-final /n/, which some have also suggested as being of African origin (Otheguy 1975, Guy 1981; also Alvarez Nazario 1974). Certainly, /s/, /l/ and /r/ are most severely reduced in precisely those areas of Latin America where the African presence was strongest and most persistent: the entire Caribbean region, including the Antilles and coastal Central and South America, and the northern Pacific coast of South America. Word-final /n/ is also velarized in these areas, but also throughout all of southeastern Mexico and Central America, in nearly all of Ecuador and much of Peru and Bolivia; /d/ and /r/ are only infrequently neutralized in Latin America, principally along the Pacific coast of Colombia and Ecuador, and in parts of the Dominican Republic. In those regions where an early African presence was later offset by indigenous influences or massive European immigration, the consonants in question are more resistant to reduction and modification; these areas include central Mexico, highland Colombia and Bolivia, and the Southern Cone nations. In every area of Latin America which exhibits these consonantal reductions, a significant African population was present during a significant portion of the colonial era (Alvarez Nazario 1974, Canfield 1981, Lipski 1985c; b, g).

Unfortunately for this apparent orderliness, most of the same consonantal modifications are found, at times in more advanced state, throughout all of southern and western Spain and the Canary Islands, and are responsible for the well-known Andalusian theories of Latin American Spanish. According to the most coherent and well-documented theories, the Andalusian phonetic influence was strongest in major port areas, in close contact with Spanish fleets, sailors, stevedores and other workers (Menéndez Pidal 1962). Precisely these same port areas were the principal receiving points in the slave trade, and became the centers of the largest and most permanent African populations in Latin America: Havana, Santo Domingo, Portobelo, Cartagena, Guayaquil, and numerous smaller ports. Only in Lima, Peru and Veracruz and Acapulco, Mexico were the strong African influences subsequently diluted by other tendencies, while the ports of Chile, Argentina, Uruguay and Paraguay came into prominence later, when the possible Andalusian influences were already tempered by other evolutionary forces. Thus it is difficult, if not impossible, to separate the two sets of variables: possible African influences and Andalusian characteristics, at least if only demographic data are used as evidence (Lipski 1986). In the background, there remains the question of creole Portuguese substrata to further complicate the reconstruction of earlier stages of colonial American Spanish. Let us therefore consider the three possible configurations described earlier, in the light of recent work in Afro-Hispanic linguistics; we begin with the possible existence of Afro-Hispanic creole dialects in which creole Portuguese and pan-American bozal Spanish elements are negligible or totally absent.

The first group to be considered are the *negros congos* of the *costa arriba* or eastern Caribbean coast of Panama, from Portobelo eastward to Miramar (Drolet 1980, Joly 1981, Zárate 1962, Lipski 1985b). Portobelo is of great historical importance, since it was for several centuries one of the major Atlantic ports of the Spanish Main, and, together with Cartagena and Veracruz, one of the few ports authorized for the importation of African slaves. Later abandoned by the Spaniards due to repeated pirate attacks, Portobelo degenerated into a sleepy community of a few hundred inhabitants, and until only a few years ago was cut off from the rest of Panama except by sea.

Up the coast from Portobelo is Nombre de Dios, the first Spanish port in Panama, abandoned even earlier than Portobelo, and yet another Palenque, derived from but not identical with an earlier community of escaped slaves or *cimarrones*. Unlike the residents of Colombia's Palenque, the inhabitants of Panama's costa arriba do not speak a Spanish creole as a home language, although the percentage of lexical Africanisms is rather high; their language is typical of rural uneducated Panamanian and Caribbean Spanish. There does exist, however, a peculiar subculture in this area known as the *negros congos*, a name derived from a ritual replayed each year during Carnival season, in which each town designates a group of congos whose leaders, Juan de Dioso and La Reina, construct a *rancho* or shack and defend it from mock attacks from congo groups of neighboring settlements. The congo ritual is elaborate and contains a rich heritage of African traditions, including dancing, singing and drumming; at the same time, there is a stylized dramatic reenactment of the life of African slaves in Colonial Panama, including the existence of congo "kingdoms" and slave uprisings.

Of interest to the linguist is a form of speaking associated with the rituals, the so-called *hablar en congo*, which may provide a window into earlier Africanized pidgin and creole patterns in this area. Many residents of Portobelo and some in the easternmost communities claim not to be fluent in congo dialect, although nearly all understand it, and certain individuals are recognized virtuosi in this mode of speaking. Costeños frequently indicate that this dialect is only used during Carnival season, but this is not entirely accurate, since daily interaction at a personal level is often punctuated with congo dialect elements, and residents of the costa arriba, when travelling to Colón or Panama City, may speak to each other in the dialect, to impede being overheard and to distinguish themselves from black descendants of West Indians (known as *afroantillanos* in Panama), whom they feel to be inferior to legitimate descendants of colonial slaves (*afrocoloniales*).

On the surface, congo speech appears to be a modern imitation of bozal Spanish of earlier centuries, and yet the congo tradition is unbroken from the present time as far back as the regional oral history itself, which includes events occurring over a period of more than 200 years. Nowadays, the element of ritual and burlesque is foremost in congo speech, which is a prime example of play language as studied by anthropologists in other areas of the world. In this dimension, congo speech is loosely constrained by rules, less rigid than Pig Latin, Spanish *jerigonza* and similar verbal games. During the congo games, the dramatic players put old clothes on inside out, originally a mockery of finely dressed Spanish colonial administrators, who donated cast-off clothing to slaves and allowed them to "dress up" during the annual *feria* at Portobelo. Taking advantage of the double meaning of Spanish *al revés* as both "inside out" and "backwards," the congo players improvise speech so that many words receive the opposite meaning: *muerto* 'dead' becomes *vivi* 'alive,' *monte* 'up in the hills' becomes *ciudad* 'the city,' *sentarse* 'to sit down' becomes *padase* 'to stand up,' and so forth. Words are phonetically and morphologically deformed in a more or less improvized fashion, often mixing gender and number; *compañero* ⇒ *cumpuñede* 'friend,' *botella vacía* ⇒ *botije llene* 'empty bottle,' *corazón* ⇒ *codajozón* 'heart,' *mañana* ⇒ *muguña* 'morning,' etc.

In other respects, congo speech resembles Cockney rhyming slang, requiring a prior initiation in order to understand certain key words, such as *macha* for *esposa* 'wife,' *agua sodilla* (*agua de chorillo*) for *aguardiente* 'liquor,' *pingadilla/pringadigui* for *cigarillo* 'cigarette,' *maripoto* for *botella* 'bottle,' *bosonilla* for *copa* 'liquor glass.' There are also a number of lexical items of possible but unverified African origin, which are not used in the local Spanish dialect and are unknown outside of the costa arriba region; these include *fuda* 'rum, liquor,' *juduminga/judumingue* 'child,' *mojobrio/mojongo* 'woman, wife,' *sopodín* 'small boat or motorized vehicle,' *potoñá* 'to leave,' *dumia* 'to eat,' *mucuna* 'the congo dialect,' *jotá* 'to smoke,' and several others. Finally, and most importantly for Afro-Hispanic creole studies, the syntax is greatly simplified, most prepositions are eliminated and noun and adjective agreement all but disappears.

These latter features are common to most Romance-based creoles; at the same time, congo dialect does not reduce all verbs to the infinitive, does not use temporal/aspectual particles such as *ta* in conjunction with the infinitive, does not reduce pronominal paradigms to a single variant (usually a stressed object pronoun) such as *mí* (e.g. *mí ta come* 'I am eating'), shows no evidence of the second-person singular pronoun *vos* (which is found in some rural regions of Panama), does not use subject pronouns as possessives (e.g. *madre mí/madre yo* 'my mother'), and does not form noun plurals by postposing the third-person plural pronoun (e.g. Papiamentu *hende* 'person,' *hendenan* 'people'). In these respects, and in other more subtle cases, congo speech suggests the existence of both an earlier pidgin or creole stage, and significant departures from Afro-Lusitanian patterns found in Papiamentu, Colombian palenquero, 19th century Caribbean bozal Spanish and the principal Portuguese creoles of Africa and Asia. This gives strength to polygenetic theories of Romance-based creoles, in at least admitting the possibility that creolized Spanish dialects may have spontaneously developed in several locations, rather than by relexification of a Portuguese-based creole.

In the phonological dimension, the congo dialect is also distinguished from prevailing Afro-Hispanic patterns. The consonants /l/, /r/, /r̄/ and /d/ are neutralized in word-initial and intervocalic position, not in favor of [r] but of the occlusive [d]: *arriba* ⇒ *adiba* 'up,' *cara* ⇒ *cada* 'face,' *lente* ⇒ *dente* 'lens.' Syllable-final /s/, /l/ and /r/ are normally lost, but this is characteristic of the regional Spanish dialect as well, as is velarization of word-final /n/. The only item in congo speech which shows any noticeable similarity with Portuguese-based creoles is the occasional shift of /Cl/ ⇒ /Cr/: *claro* ⇒ *crado* 'of course,' *diablo* ⇒ *diabria* 'devil,' *clavo* ⇒ *cravo* 'nail'; however, this change has been observed in areas of Spain far removed from Portuguese influence (e.g. Salvador Salvador 1978), and such spontaneous generation cannot be ruled out in the isolated and socially marginalized costa arriba. Portobelo and the rest of the costa arriba represents the last vestiges of a post-creole continuum, since there are no monolingual speakers of congo dialect, nor have there been for as long as the local oral tradition has existed; it is doubtful whether any two residents could speak entirely in congo for a long period of time since Spanish has become inextricably mixed with the earlier pidgin/creole patterns. An example of congo speech (Lipski 1985b: 40) is:

> *pedo yo dije que yo te venía buhco, y te dije aquí mineda fue pa con ehta, pedo dije no voy a sadime poque pueden darme un . . . un tido, yo te dije pédame que tengo mi cumpromiso contigo . . . bueno, aquí me midas, ¿qué quedes? Ponga en órbito, ahoda te acuedda que, ahoda somo loh dos,*

¿sabo? Gruya, ¿tú midahte ese poco de macha que había en ese dao? ['but I said I would come for you, I told you that was my plan, but I said I won't go out because they could... shoot me, I told you to wait for me because I had a commitment; now here I am; what do you want? Let's get started, remember there are two of us now. Gruya, did you see that bunch of women there?']

Another region of possible significance for the separation of variables in Afro-Hispanic studies is the Chota Valley, which contains a small Afro-American population in highland Ecuador (Lipski c, h). Although Ecuador is not one of the Latin American areas normally associated with large African populations, the Afro-Ecuadoran component may be as high as 25% of the national total. The majority of the black and mulatto population is concentrated in the northwest sector, principally in Esmeraldas province, where over 80% of the residents are of African descent. The origin of Ecuador's black population is surrounded by some controversy, since although it is evident that black Ecuadorans arrived from the north, dates of arrival and region of origin have yet to be determined satisfactorily.[4] One theory, as yet unproved, maintains that the first permanent black residents arrived on the Ecuadoran coast as the result of a shipwreck at the end of the 16th century, and another in 1600, although it is known that the first blacks arrived in Ecuador in 1533–1536. Subsequently, the Jesuits were responsible for large-scale importation of black slaves to work on plantations both on the coast and in the central highlands, and this example was followed by other planters and landowners, since indigenous labor was scarce in certain areas and rebellious in many others. Early in the 19th century, the wars of colonial liberation brought contingents of black soldiers to Ecuador, coming mostly from Colombia, and when manumission of slaves took place in Ecuador in 1852, many of these black subjects remained in Esmeraldas province. Yet another group of black citizens arrived in the late 19th century, when some 4000–5000 Jamaican laborers were brought to work on plantations and on construction projects; this was the last significant migration of Afro-Americans to Ecuador. Other scholars have maintained that the black population of Esmeraldas province results from the immigration of laborers from plantations in the central highlands; this theory, however, is difficult to reconcile with the historical and demographic facts of colonial and post-colonial Ecuador. It also leaves unanswered the ultimate origin of blacks in highland Ecuador.

In the highlands, the predominant racial type is the indigenous or mestizo configuration, and black or mulatto residents are quite rare. The one exception is the Chota River valley and its environs, in the north-central provinces of Imbabura and Carchi. This valley, formerly known as Coangue, is a tropi-

---

[4] A composite of historical and linguistic sources on the Chota Valley includes: Estupiñán Tello (1967: 45–8), Toscano Mateus (1953: 19–20), Rout (1976: 211–32), Wolf (1892: 525), Whitten (1965: 22–5; 1974: 179), Peaherrera de Costales and Costales Samaniego (1959), Klumpp (1970), Coba Andrade (1980: 19–49), Whitten and Friedemann (1974).

cal lowland surrounded by Andean uplands, and the population of the Chota region is almost entirely black with some mulattoes, in contrast to the exclusively indigenous/mestizo population of neighboring areas. The Chota valley consists of some 10–15 small villages, with a variable population that probably does not exceed a total of 15,000. The origin of this black population in highland Ecuador is also surrounded by uncertainty; some investigators have suggested that choteños are descended from freed or escaped slaves from the coast, but it appears that most blacks in Imbabura and Carchi provinces are descendants of slaves held by the Jesuits on their highland plantations (and also, according to some evidence, in slave breeding centers). Up until the middle of the 18th century, the wealth of the Jesuit order was considerable in Ecuador, and in Carchi and Imbabura province the order owned a number of sugar plantations. Many of these estates still exist, as do the settlements that arose around them, and when the Jesuits were expelled from Ecuador in 1767, most of these slaves simply changed masters, as the lands were taken over by Ecuadoran owners. These slaves and freedmen came to form the population nuclei of the Chota valley. In the Chota valley, oral traditions only make reference to the fact that the first black residents arrived from other unspecified lands, while in Esmeraldas there is no collective awareness of any immigration from the highlands to the coast, despite the fact that some historians have traced the black coastal population to the immigration of choteños from the highlands.

When slavery was abolished in Ecuador, in 1852, the choteños continued working on the large landholdings that form the economic backbone of the region. Although it is possible that subsequent migrations may have brought black residents from the coast, the majority of the choteños share a history of more than 250 years of residence in the central highlands. It is not impossible that black choteños had subsequent contact with coastal speech modes, but given the isolation of the Chota Valley, the poor communication with the coast and the overwhelming linguistic influence of the surrounding highland dialects, this population is perhaps the only significant black settlement in Spanish America without close and recent ties to life and language of the coastal lowlands.

Ecuador is rarely mentioned in the context of creole Spanish; however, some indirect evidence exists which suggests that in previous centuries a creole or bozal Spanish may have been spoken among certain groups of Afro-Ecuadorans, particularly those living in isolated communities or cimarrón societies (Chávez Franco 1930:524–9, Granda 1978:381–3). In Esmeraldas province, where the majority of Ecuador's black population is concentrated, the local Spanish dialect is by no means creolized, although it is decidedly popular, with the costeño phonetic characteristics found throughout Latin America. Some researchers have claimed that in the jungle villages in the interior of the province, a "special" Spanish dialect is still spoken, or was spoken until not long ago (Estupiñán Tello 1967: 49). More recently, I have been able to personally verify that the "special" dialects are merely popular variants of Spanish, and contain no creole traits. The Spanish dialect of the Chota valley has never been the object of serious linguistic investigation, although some indirect testimony suggests that in the past this dialect may have exhibited creole or at least highly nonstandard tendencies when compared with the other dialect zones of Ecuador, although presently the choteño dialect is not a creole. This does not preclude the prior existence of partially Africanized Spanish in the Chota region, as will be seen shortly, but it does set back the dates for the gradual decreolization which would have given rise to the present popular but noncreolized choteño Spanish, and casts a large measure of doubt on casual observations by Ecuadorans and foreigners with regard to the "deformed" and "unintelligible" speech of blacks.

In the provinces of Imbabura and the southern portion of Carchi, including the Chota valley, the linguistic characteristics belong to general highland Ecuadoran Spanish; in particular, word-final /n/ is velarized, syllable-final consonants are resistant to neutralization and effacement, word-final prevocalic /s/ is frequently pronounced as [z] (e.g. *los amigos* [*lozamigos*] 'the friends'), and unstressed vowels may fall in contact with /s/. The only major deviations are found among indigeneous subjects who are not fluent in Spanish; the dialect of the black choteños in general shares the features of this dialect zone, rather than those of the coastal black and nonblack populations, whose speech is characterized by typical "coastal" pronunciation, including loss of implosive /s/ and /r/ and neutralization of implosive /l/ and /r/.

The behavior of /s/ is of particular interest in the Chota dialect (Lipski c), since in general it falls more nearly in line with the highland dialects, in retaining the sibilant [s], but the percentage of aspiration and loss (13%) is significantly higher than in other highland dialects, including nearby towns in Imbabura and Carchi provinces. Substantially the same is true for word-final preconsonantal and prevocalic /s/, whose phonetic parameters are virtually identical to the previous case, and where the Chota dialect does reduce /s/ to a greater degree (19% as compared to 4-5%) than in other highland zones). The most significant discrepancies come in phrase-final position, where the Chota dialect weakens or deletes /s/ to a notably greater degree than in neighboring highland dialects. These quantitative differences may not seem important, particularly when compared to the nearly categorical reduction of /s/ in the Esmeraldas region, but the black Chota dialect stands out clearly from its highland neighbors where loss of /s/ (with the exception of the word *entonces*, frequently pronounced without final /s/ in all of Ecuador) is so rare as to immediately call attention to even a single case of loss of phrase-final /s/. The noncategorical nature of the reduction of /s/ in the Chota dialect indicates that the process is not purely phonetically motivated, as it is in the coastal dialects. In many cases, word-final /s/ is lost in the choteño dialect when it is not morphologically significant, and is retained when it is an essential part of nominal or verbal inflections. This is the type of configuration to be expected in the last stages of decreolization (or for that matter, in incipient creolization), where grammatical endings have largely been restored, but where the tendency to ignore grammatically irrelevant endings has not been totally overcome. With respect to the pronunciation of /s/, the Chota dialect differs from neighboring highland dialects, and suggests the possible existence of earlier pronunciation patterns among the black highlanders.

In addition to the rather subtle phonetic/phonological dimension, the black Chota dialect manifests some syntactic divergence from other Ecuadoran dialects, particularly among the area's oldest and/or least educated residents, whose speech patterns have been least influenced by non-choteño Spanish. In the area of grammatical concordance, particularly between nouns and adjectives, and between subjects and predicates, Chota Valley Spanish exhibits subtle but noticeable differences from other Ecuadoran dialects, where discrepancies of agreement are rare among monolingual Spanish speakers and fluent bilinguals.

Examples gleaned from the Chota Valley include:

se trabajaban[-0] en las haciendas vecino[-as]
'people worked in the near-by plantations'

sobre la materia mismo[-a] de cada pueblo
'with the materials from each town'

era barato[-a] la ropa, barato era
'clothes were cheap'

hay gente colombiano[-a]
'there are people from Colombia'

Lack of concordance in verb phrases also occurs, as does loss of the reflexive pronoun *se* and occasional confusion of the copulative verbs *ser* and *estar*:

chota [se] compone con [de], compone dos sequíos, se llaman un pueblo.
'The town called Chota is composed of two portions.'

estamos [somos] 17 comunidades
'We are 17 communities [in all].'

últimamente la gente [se] está [de-]dicando a la agricultura
'Lately, the people have turned to agriculture.'

comienza[-n] a colorearse las vistas
'Their eyes start to get red.'

se pone[-n] lo[-s] guagua medios[-0] mal de cuerpo, se ponen amarillos
'The babies get very sick, they turn yellow.'

Errors of prepositional usage are also rather frequent, consisting of elimination of certain common prepositions, and interchange of others:

yo soy [de] abajo
'I'm from down the road.'

depende [de] las posibilidades del padre
'It depends on the father's possibilities.'

San Lorenzo que queda muy cerca con [de] la Concepción
'San Lorenzo, which is very near La Concepción'

Also found is the occasional elimination of articles, which is rarely found in other Ecuadoran dialects, among monolingual Spanish speakers:

porque [el] próximo pueblo puede ser Salinas
'because the next town could be Salinas'

material de aquí de[l] lugar
'material from around here'

Finally, there are some examples which, in terms of significant syntactic deviance, fall more in line with creolized Spanish from other areas of Latin America, and from past centuries:

con yerbas de campo curaban a nosotros [nos curaban]
'They cured us with country herbs.'

a poca costumbre se la tiene [??] cuando mucha [muy] fuerte está la fiebre
'It's difficult when the fever is very high.'

casi lo más lo más lo tocan guitarra y bomba [lo que más tocan son la guitarra y la bomba]
'Mostly what they play are guitars and bombas.'

The above constructions, which occur relatively frequently in the Chota Valley dialect, are virtually unknown in their totality in other Ecuadoran Spanish dialects, although individual examples may at times be heard elsewhere.

An overall comparison between the grammatical characteristics of choteño Spanish and known Afro-Hispanic manifestations from other regions and from past time periods, reveals certain structural similarities and strategies which suggest that in its earliest stages, black highland Ecuadoran Spanish shared some of the features of bozal/African Spanish of other regions. The study of the speech of black choteños, who have lived in highland Ecuador for 250 years, suggests an earlier stage when partially Africanized Spanish was generally spoken in the Chota Valley. This is significant in postulating the use of partially creolized Spanish away from the Caribbean "heartland" in which most such dialects are to be found, and because the choteños have always coexisted linguistically with non-African neighbors, and were never part of a resistance movement or cimarrón society. The surviving remnants of this language follow general patterns of creole language behavior, although no traces of putative Portuguese creole are found.

Turning to Afro-Hispanic contacts which failed to produce configurations associated with creole and bozal Spanish, the case of Equatorial Guinea is foremost. Equatorial Guinea is unique in being the only officially Spanish-speaking region in sub-Saharan Africa, and it is the only area in black Africa where Spanish has ever been spoken on a regular basis.[5] This nation, which was known as Spanish Guinea until its independence in 1968, consists of the island territory of Fernando Poo (Bioko) and the mainland enclave of Río Muni, between Gabon and Cameroon, as well as several small islands, the most important of which is Annobon, whose residents speak a Portuguese-derived creole similar to that of São Tomé. Although Spain held Fernando Poo since the middle of the 18th century, serious colonization was not begun until the last decades of the 19th century, while Río Muni was settled only after the turn of the 20th century. Thus, the Spanish language is a relatively recent arrival in this territory, in comparison with European languages as used in neighboring nations. Despite the relatively recent date of Spanish presence in Equatorial Guinea, the Spanish language has been effectively implanted as the official medium of communication, set against the background of the still vigorous native languages, being principally Bubi on Fernando Poo and Fang and the *playero* languages in Río Muni.

On Fernando Poo, Pidgin English is widely spoken, being originally brought by the descendants of laborers from Sierra Leone and Liberia who were brought to Fernando Poo in the last century, and more recently by the thousands of Nigerian contract laborers who worked on the cacao plantations. Spanish is not spoken as a true native language by Equatorial Guineans except in a few cases of mixed-ethnic marriages, but all Guineans living in the cities and larger rural communities learn Spanish as the result of an effective educational system which was set up by the Spanish government in conjunction with several religious orders. Only Spanish is used in official communications, on the radio and in government offices, although the ver-

---

5 The principal sources for Guinean Spanish, which include a complete bibliography, are: González Echegaray (1959), Granda (1984, 1985), Lipski (1984, 1985a, 1986).

naculars are generally preferred in daily transactions, liberally mixed with Spanish elements. It is unlikely that Spanish will die out in Equatorial Guinea, since it provides the only bridge between traditionally hostile ethnic groups, and since it represents a symbol of national identity vis-à-vis the neighboring French-, English- and Portuguese-speaking nations of the Gulf of Guinea. During the unfortunate regime which governed the country for the first eleven years following independence, massive population shifts were forced upon the people, which had the effect of reinforcing the use of Spanish (as well as Pidgin English and Fang) as a means of communication between groups who spoke different languages. Currently there is no official position regarding public language usage, but the example set by the government openly favors Spanish, in the face of the lack of viable alternatives. The Spanish government campaigned against the use of Pidgin English, but the current Equatorial Guinean government appears to accept use of this language as a commercial vehicle useful in dealing with neighboring countries.

The Spanish as spoken in Equatorial Guinea has a definite and unmistakable "African accent" both in terms of phonetics and intonation and in terms of grammar and vocabulary, and yet the most noteworthy feature is that it is not creolized or pidginized, nor is there evidence that a creole stage ever existed. A pidgin stage evidently did exist, following the initial introduction of Spanish into the territory, but was soon followed by the formation of reasonably stable local varieties of Spanish. Language proficiency among Equatorial Guineans ranges from a low degree for a small percentage of speakers to a surprising degree of fluency, which approaches that of native monolingual speakers. At the same time, even the most educated Guineans occasionally commit slight but noticeable grammatical errors with respect to usage in other Spanish-speaking areas, and none has overcome the peculiar segmental and suprasegmental modality of Guinean Spanish. In answer to why creolization has not taken place, we consider the normally accepted preconditions for creolization and discover that many do not obtain in Equatorial Guinea:

(1) Guineans have never been removed from contact with native speakers of Spanish for prolonged periods of time. Except for the final years of the previous xenophobic regime, Equatorial Guinea received a constant influx of Spaniards and boasted a sizable resident Spanish population. Thus Guinean society was divided into those members who interacted constantly with the Spaniards and those few who due to geographical isolation had little contact with Spaniards and who learned little Spanish. To this may be added the increasingly effective language instruction available to Guineans in larger population centers and in most rural areas.

(2) There is little evidence for the "baby talk" aspect of creolization, since there is no record of Spaniards' consistently simplifying their speech

in order to communicate with Guineans. To the contrary, most Spaniards in Equatorial Guinea have used full forms of the language, even when this results in noticeable lack of total understanding among Guineans.

(3) While at times some Spanish colonizers and plantation owners may have treated Guinean workers less than generously, slavery never existed in this territory, and the contacts between Guineans and Spaniards were marked by a different set of structural parameters than in the Spanish American colonies.

(4) Most importantly, there was never a massive fragmentation or dispersion of Guinean ethnic groups which would have forced Spanish into the position of the only mutually comprehensible medium of communication. Equatorial Guineans have always been able to use their own languages for purposes of daily communication, combined with Pidgin English in the multiethnic communities on Fernando Poo, and until the genocidal attempts of the previous regime there was often little need for Guineans to speak to fellow citizens in Spanish.

The current political environment is resulting in a reconcentration of ethnic groups, but when Guineans do communicate with other compatriots in Spanish the results, while often grammatically and lexically simplified, do not give evidence of pidginization. Added to this factor is the fact that radio broadcasting has always used Spanish, although there are currently a few hours of daily programming in the indigenous languages, and newspapers and official publications have used only Spanish. The linguistic and cultural distance from European Spanish never became so great as to result in a cutoff of the sort that occurred in many other African and Caribbean regions, although one is free to speculate on the linguistic effects that would have occurred after 100 or more years of cultural isolation such as attempted by the previous government. A certain element of linguistic nationalism may also be at work, since Equatorial Guinea, with its checkered history, is a Spanish-speaking enclave in the midst of English-, French-, Portuguese- and creole-speaking nations, and Equatorial Guineans, long accustomed to exile and job hunting in neighboring countries, find that clinging to Spanish provides the only mark of national identity. A noteworthy feature of the speech of most Equatorial Guineans, especially when speaking to "Europeans" but even when conversing among themselves in Spanish, is the attention to correction and precision, the self-conscious striving for linguistic accuracy which bears a striking resemblance to the performance of conscientious foreign language students. Equatorial Guineans are proud of their ability to speak Spanish, including those who speak the language less than perfectly, and even 'off the record' conversations reveal self-conscious corrections, amendments and additions, virtually nonexistent among monolingual native Spanish speakers in other countries, as well as hypercorrections and malapropisms.

Phonetically, Guinean Spanish has intonational patterns radically different from those of Peninsular Spanish, maintains /b/, /d/ and /g/ as stops in all contexts, and separates individual words by a slight pause or glottal stop. However, in terms of the consonantal variables most frequently associated with Africanist theories of Spanish dialectology, the results are somewhat unexpected. The only pan-African phonetic trait is the neutralization of the single tap /r/ and the multiple trill /r̄/ in favor of [r]. The liquids /l/ and /r/ are never neutralized, there is no interchange of /d/ and /r/, word-final /n/ is uniformly alveolar, despite the fact that many of the indigenous languages contain word-final velar /n/. Finally, syllable-final /s/ is resistant, never becoming aspirated and only occasionally being elided, and then only in cases of morphological redundancy. Although the indigenous Equatorial Guinean languages come from the same families as those represented among the African populations of Spanish America, and despite the lack of consonantal desinences in the Guinean languages, Equatorial Guinean Spanish is remarkably free of consonantal reductions, in comparison with "Africanized" Latin American dialects. One may question the possible role of the educational system on the relative recentness of the Spanish language in Africa and of the nonfragmentation of Guinean ethnic groups, but the most important factor in determining the characteristics of Equatorial Guinean Spanish is the dialect base brought from Spain. The majority of Spaniards who lived and worked in Spanish Guinea were Catalans and Valencians, with a lesser number coming from northern and Central Spain (Castile). In other words, the Spanish as spoken by the majority of Spaniards in Equatorial Guinea was characterized by

(1) maintenance of syllable-final /s/ as a sibilant [s];

(2) realization of word-final /n/ as alveolar [n];

(3) lack of neutralization of /l/ and /r/;

(4) variable incorporation of the interdental phoneme /θ/.

In the phonological dimension, then, the dialect base of Guinean Spanish is radically different from the Andalusian and Canarian dialects which circulated among the Spanish American coastal regions which were also characterized by significant African populations. Guinean Spanish serves as a test case not only for theories of pidginization and creolization of Spanish, but also of the necessary contribution of African languages to "Caribbean" phonological patterns, since while the native languages of Equatorial Guinea have almost no instances of syllable-final /s/, /l/ and /r/ and frequently velarize word-final /n/, modification of these consonants was not present in the received Spanish pronunciation, and did not penetrate into the newly emerging Guinean Spanish. This partial separation of the African language variable and the Spanish dialect base indicates that the presence of African languages is in itself not sufficient to trigger the wholesale consonantal modifications found in Caribbean Spanish. This in turn gives weight to the more moderate hypothesis that African speakers in Spanish America imitated and extended the already weakened consonantal articulations of the regional Spanish dialects found in many port and coastal regions of the New World. Some examples of Equatorial Guinean Spanish are (Lipski 1985a: 25-9):

> *yo no vivo de [en] Malabo, yo soy de Bata y vive [vivo] ahí*
> 'I'm not from Malabo, I'm from Bata and I live there.'
>
> *entonces ellos preguntó [preguntaron]*
> 'then they asked'
>
> *¿cómo voy [va] a asustarme el frío de allí?*
> 'How could the cold there frighten me?'
>
> *los fang, alguna[os] hace[n] trampa, prepá[ran] nipa*
> 'The Fang, some make traps, some prepare nipa.'
>
> *cacao hay poca[o], no hay tanto*
> 'There's only a little cacao.'

The final case to be considered is the existence of speech communities in which linguistic phenomena similar or identical to those occurring in Afro-Romance creole dialects have been produced in situations where the Afro-Lusitanian connection is demonstrably absent. The successful demonstration of such cases would indicate that while a Portuguese/African basis may be a sufficient condition for the formation of many creole languages, it is not a necessary concomitant, in that other factors may converge to produce identical results. While several possible cases immediately come to mind, the most profitable area of research lies in the domain of vestigial Spanish, as spoken by individuals and groups in which rapid language shifts away from Spanish have created configurations that strongly resemble those found in creole languages. Regardless of the wide disparity among theories of creolization, one common denominator that permeates all theoretical accounts is the deficiency of the language-learning environment, in terms of providing adequate models of native-speaker performance. It is generally postulated that pidgins and creoles are formed in the absence of sustained contact with a sufficiently large corpus of native-level linguistic material, aided by social and political policies that take a hostile or at best indifferent view towards the speakers in question and their language behavior. The other side of the coin, the gradual erosion that occurs in situations of language shift leading to language death, has rarely been studied with a view toward the similarities with creolization; nevertheless, available information points to this configuration as a significant element in the evaluation of theories of creolization. Currently, vestigial Spanish speakers are found in various areas, which share no common defining characteristics except for the existence of Spanish vestigial or "semi" speakers: the Caribbean island of Trinidad; St. Bernard Parish,

Louisiana; the Philippines; and nonfluent second and third generation Hispanic bilinguals in the United States, of Mexican, Puerto Rican and Cuban origin. The speech of these groups exhibits the following features associated with Romance-based creoles, and which have at times been cited as evidence in favor of a unique or monogenetic origin:

(1) reduction of verbal and nominal morphology;

(2) occasional neutralization of pronominal paradigms;

(3) elimination of common prepositions;

(4) elimination of articles;

(5) use of *tener* with existential force;

(6) overall reduction of syntactic complexity, especially embedded constructions;

(7) phonological reduction, incorrect word division and insecurity.

Language erosion, leading to ultimate language death, has only in the past few decades come under serious scrutiny by linguists, and the transfer mechanisms between vestigial language and "full" language usage are gradually being explored. The erosion of Spanish has usually been studied in the United States setting, and most typically has involved tracing the penetration of Anglicisms in vocabulary, structure and pronunciation, as well as general loss of fluency and manipulation of normally accepted grammatical patterns. Since much of the research has been oriented toward educational policy and language identification and maintenance, less emphasis has been placed on the processes and strategies that characterize "dying" Spanish, and more attention has been directed at speakers whose language usage is, while regarded as nonstandard, within the limits of native-speaker proficiency. A comparison of these speakers with the former groups yields radically different patterns, which while perhaps of only limited relevance to educational programs, are significant for creole studies. Within the United States, Spanish speakers of Cuban (CU), Puerto Rican (PR) and Mexican (MX) origin exhibit a continuum of linguistic proficiency, ranging from complete fluency in comparison with the countries of origin, to a nearly total lack of ability in the Spanish language. Among the latter group, loss of Spanish typically occurs during the process of transculturation, and normally involves a phase of passive bilingualism, in which children hear Spanish spoken by older relatives, while their own active linguistic production is effectively limited to English. Alternatively, a marriage between a Spanish speaker and a non-Spanish speaker may create a home environment conducive to the formation of semispeakers. Naturally, such speakers do not live in discrete geographic areas, but may be found throughout the nation, although the density of semispeakers increases in areas where no large homogeneous Hispanic populations are found. The main criterion for the existence of semispeakers is language shift within the immediate environment of the speakers in question; the variables of educational level, socioeconomic status and geographical location are of considerably less importance in determining eventual language loss.

The case of the isleños (IS) of St. Bernard Parish, Louisiana is rather special, since this group does not represent the result of recent immigration, but is rather a remnant of colonial migrations, in this case of a group of Canary Islanders who arrived in the then Spanish territory of Louisiana at the end of the 18th century (MacCurdy 1950, Guillotte 1982, Lipski f). Since the region inhabited by the isleños lies in a sparsely populated part of swampy east Louisiana, until the 1940s this group was able to maintain a certain cultural and linguistic autonomy from the rest of the state's population, and even today many members of the group cling to the traditions and life styles of previous decades. However, language shift has occurred; the youngest isleños generally have only a passive knowledge of Spanish, and many middle-aged isleños fall into the category of semispeakers, although there are still a number of speakers of fluent, if somewhat Anglicized, Spanish in this group.

Trinidad Spanish (TR) is another curious phenomenon, since this island passed from Spanish to British hands at the end of the 18th century, and the implantation of the Spanish language lasted fewer than fifty years (Moodie 1973, 1982, a; Thompson 1957). Although the island of Trinidad saw considerable immigration of Venezuelan peons in the 19th century, the number of Spanish speakers is currently only a fraction of a percent of the total population, few speakers of any level are found that are less than 50 years old, and except for a literal handful of the oldest speakers, most Spanish-speaking Trinidadians are legitimately classed in the semispeaker category. The failure to implement Spanish in any official capacity, including in the school system, has resulted in the nearly complete deterioration of the language, although through a curious set of circumstances, many Trinidadians sing Spanish-language Christmas songs, known as *parang* (from *parranda*) each year, with only a few understanding the words they sing.

Vestigial Philippine Spanish (PH) is the most peripheral case, both geographically and sociolinguistically. Although Spain held the Philippines for nearly 400 years, only a tiny percentage of Filipinos ever learned Spanish, by official design, although a Hispanic creole (Chabacano) sprang up in Zamboanga and in several points along Manila Bay (Whinnom 1954, 1956; Frake 1971; Quilis 1980, 1984; Bowen 1971; Sibayan 1971). Following the Spanish-American war, the linguistic shift to English as a second language was rapidly effected, while the campaign to make Tagalog (Pilipino) a nation-wide second language is having considerable success. Currently in the Philippines fewer than 1% of the national population claims (noncreole) Spanish as a first or second language; these speakers are nearly all from mestizo (Eurasian) families of the upper socioeconomic classes, and speak

Spanish only under limited circumstances. Few families are found which use Spanish consistently, although many claim to do so, and the desire to retain Spanish is frequently a strategy designed to reclaim the last vestiges of aristocratic prestige vis-à-vis the progressive Tagalization of the Philippines. Enough Spanish speakers remain in the Philippines, however, to constitute a pool of linguistic material, which up until now has never been adequately studied, attention always having been drawn to the creole dialects and indigenous languages. Virtually all Philippine Spanish speakers speak one or more of the national languages natively or as a strong second language, although many individuals claim no knowledge of these languages; in addition, all but the oldest speakers have at least some knowledge of English. Philippine Spanish is clearly a dying language, with almost no speakers under the age of 60 to be found, except for language teachers who learned Spanish in school or through foreign scholarships. Among the last generation of Spanish speakers, continuous variation exists from the most aristocratic and refined Peninsular Spanish (with late 19th century overtones) to a rudimentary and hesitant "semi-Spanish" only slightly more proficient than that of foreign learners. In Guam, once part of the Spanish Pacific empire, Spanish has completely disappeared, after having left significant traces on the native language, Chamorro. My survey uncovered only three speakers with any knowledge of Spanish, although a few more may exist, and all fit into the category of semispeakers (cf. also Bowen 1971, Trifonovitch 1971). The last fluent Spanish speakers disappeared from Guam more than a generation ago. A few examples of vestigial Guam Spanish (GU) have been included to indicate yet another case of language erosion in a situation of total isolation.

Let us now consider the creole-like manifestations of the various vestigial Spanish dialects under consideration. First, in the area of verbal morphology, where, in addition to the production of correct forms, the most frequent strategy is to use the third person singular verb form, i.e., the least marked; the second most common case is the use of third person plural forms for first person plural. Thus, there is a tendency for some variant of the third person to become the canonical verb form in vestigial Spanish, although this only occurs in a small proportion of the total number of conjugated verbs. In Hispanic creoles, the third person singular verb form vies with a form of the verbal infinitive for canonical status.

yo bailo y come [como]
'I dance and eat.' (MX)

viene [vienen] mis tíos del rancho d'él [de su rancho]
'My aunt and uncle come from their ranch.' (MX)

se m'olvida [olvidan] muchas palabra[s]
'I forget a lot of words.' (CU)

tó[dos] nojotro trabajaban [trabajábamos] junto[s]
'We all worked together.' (TR)

yo tiene [tengo] cuaranta ocho año
'I am 48 years old.' (TR)

asina, yo pone [pongo] todo
'I put everything like that.'(TR)

yo no sabe [sé] bien
'I don't know.' (TR)

sí, yo entiende [entiendo]
'Yes, I understand.' (IS)

ahí todos eh [son] raza isleña
'There they are all isleños.' (IS)

Nosotro saben [sabemos] trabajá junto
'We know how to work together.' (IS)

Por aquí entra [entran] los barcos internacionales
'The international ships enter here.' (PH)

Cuando vino [vinieron] los japoneses
'when the Japanese came' (PH)

Los padres españoles, aquellos [ellos] habla [hablan] buen [bien] en chamorro
'The Spanish priests, they spoke Chamorro well.' (GU)

These examples are notably similar to those reported for bozal Spanish of previous centuries, and for presently occurring Afro-Hispanic dialect pockets. In addition to the examples from Equatorial Guinea and Ecuador, other cases come from Samaná, Dominican Republic (González and Benavides 1982):

supongo que debe [debo] tener 60 años
'I guess I'm 60 years old';

from 19th century Puerto Rican bozal Spanish (Alvarez Nazario 1974: 386; Mason and Espinosa 1927: 410):

yo dicí a ti [yo te digo]
'I'm telling you';

> *ese [esa] Nazaria son [es] mugé mala*
> 'That Nazario is a bad woman.'

Bozal Spanish from previous centuries provides similar examples. From Lope de Rueda (1908), in the 16th century, comes:

> *mas ¿sabe qué querer [quiere] yo?*
> 'But do you know what I want?'

Diego de Badajoz wrote, in the same century (Barrantes 1882):

> *¿Quen dis [dice] aquí tene [tiene] pan?*
> 'Who is said to have bread here?'

Góngora (1980) offered

> *La alma sá [las almas son] como la denta [los dientes]*
> 'Souls are like teeth.

In all of these examples, the strategy represented by the verbal instability is the same: partial use of verbal conjugations, with a general gravitation toward the third person singular forms as the most "unmarked."

The second category is reduction of nominal morphology. In the vestigial Spanish dialects under study, reduction and neutralization of nominal and adjectival gender is frequent, and takes the form of nonetymological gender or number assignment to particular lexical items, or of inconsistent use of gender and number morphemes across a single noun phrase. While the most common outcome is the maximally unmarked masculine singular, which normally forms the basis for creole adjectives and articles, other less systematic substitutions also occur, at times reflecting uncertainty as to the gender of morphologically opaque nouns.

> *mi blusa es blanco [blanca]*
> 'My blouse is white.' (MX)

> *tenemos un [una] casa allá*
> 'We have a house there.' (MX)

> *¿cuál es tu favorito [favorita] parte?*
> 'What is your favorite part?' (CU)

> *decían palabras que eran inglés [inglesas]*
> 'They said words that were [in] English.' (PR)

> *ehta décima fue composío [compuesta] pol mi tío*
> 'This décima was composed by my uncle' (IS)

> *un[a] rata asina*
> 'a muskrat this big' (IS)

> *ahora tiene casa[s] uno [una] sobre otro [otra]*
> 'Now there are houses one on top of another' (TR)

> *no quieren ser español[es]*
> 'they don't want to be Spanish' (PH)

> *En estos días no hay escuela[s] español [españolas]*
> 'These days there are no Spanish schools' (GU)

The examples presented in the preceding section indicate the existence of nominal instability in creole Spanish, and of contemporary Afro-Hispanic language, employing exactly the same patterns of partial neutralization of gender and number inflection. In the Spanish Golden Age, Góngora wrote:

> *samo negra pecandora e branca la Sacramenta [somos negras pecadoras y el Sacramento es blanco]*
> 'We are black sinners and the Sacrament is white.'

Lope de Rueda wrote:

> *ya tenemo un [una] prima mía*
> 'now we have a cousin...'

The third category, modification and reduction of pronominal paradigms, is rarely manifested in vestigial Spanish dialects. In the vestigial dialects under study, radical shifts of pronominal case are extremely infrequent. Only a handful are found in the present corpus. From Trinidad, comes:

> *Si pa mí tocaba [si yo tocara] un cuatro, yo no volví [volvía a] cantá*
> 'If I knew how to play the cuatro, I wouldn't sing any more'

> *la salga eh buena pa uté [su/de usted] cabeza*
> 'sarga is good for headaches [good for your head].'

From Guam, we have:

> *los pobres samorro [chamorros], como a mí [yo]*
> 'the poor Chamorros, like me'

Neutralization and elimination of prepositions is extremely frequent in vestigial and creole Spanish dialects; the most frequent case is the elimination of the prepositions *de* and *a*, whose semantic value can frequently be reconstructed from the surrounding context. Also found is the substitution of prepositions, particularly among those which accompany specific verbs; this is ordinarily done in a nonsystematic fashion. Examples include the following.

¿Tienes oportunidades en [para] hablar el español?
'Do you have opportunities to speak Spanish?' (CU)

a casa [de] loh muchacho
'at the boys' house' (IS)

ya recibirá carta [de] Ehpaña
'I will get a letter from Spain.' (IS)

hay un poco [de] cacao
'There's a little cacao.' (TR)

bahtante fueron diferente lugal [a diferentes lugares]
'Many went to different places.' (TR)

si uté pasa [la] casa [de] Lilí
'if you pass Lili's house'(TR)

comenzaba [en] setiembre
'It began in September.' (IS)

hoy etamo [a] siete
'Today is the 7th.' (PR)

mi yerno es descendiente [de] italiano
'My son-in-law is descended from Italians.' (PH)

los empleados [de] gobierno en tiempos de Hoover
'government employees during Hoover's time' (GU)

Afro-Hispanic and other creole dialects exhibit similar behavior of prepositions, especially loss of *de* and *a*.

Reduction of syntactic complexity through elimination of embedded constructions (normally in violation of generally accepted syntactic norms) is a frequent feature of vestigial Spanish dialects:

[cuanto] más nombres [haya] mejor se va [a] ver
'The more names there are, the better it will look' (MX)

hay muchah manera loh muchacho salí [para que los muchachos salgan]
'there are many ways for the boys to go out' (IS)

tú tiene [cuando tú tengas] tiempo, viene[s] aquí
'when you have time, come back here' (TR)

la gente aquí [que] hablaron [hablaba] español se murieron
'the people here who could speak Spanish all died' (TR)

lo quieren quitar y a no ser [que no sea] obligatorio
'they want to remove it and not have it be obligatory' (PH)

antes tú que llegarte [antes que tú llegues] al monumento
'before you get to the monument' (PH)

es uno de los idiomas [que] enseñan aquí
'it's one of the languages that they teach here' (PH)

hay [había] muchos [que] bebimos tuba
'there were many of us who drank tuba [palm wine]' (GU)

Such constructions are also found in creole Spanish, as may be seen by comparing the cases already presented.

Another fundamental feature of many creole dialects, also shared by vestigial Spanish, is the elimination of articles, particularly definite articles, in cases where fluent native speakers would employ them:

cuando tú deja [la] música
'when you give up music' (PR)

[la] crihtofina cogió [el] puehto del cacao
'cristofina took the place of cacao' (TR)

no ponen [los] zapato en la mesa
'they don't put their shoes on the table' (IS)

[el] español es muy bonita[o]
'Spanish is beautiful' (PR)

me gusta[n] [las] clases como pa escribín[r]
'I like classes like writing' (CU)

tengo miedo de [los] exámen[e]s
'I'm afraid of exams' (MX)

está arriba, fuera de [del] tráfico
'it's high up, away from the traffic' (PH)

> *antes, [las] mujeres solas podíamos caminar por las Ramblas*
> 'before, women could walk alone through Las Ramblas'(PH)

A good example from bozal Spanish comes from the 19th century Peruvian novel, *Matalaché* (López Albújar 1966: 38):

> *[la] negra Casilda no moletá, amita, ella ayudao matá [la] cabrita [de] José Manué*
> 'Negra Casilda isn't angry ma'am; she helped kill José Manuel's goat.'

Another point of convergence between vestigial Spanish and bozal/Africanized Spanish, is the frequent use of redundant subject pronouns, particularly *yo, tú, usted, nosotros,* and *ustedes.* Since use of redundant pronouns is never strictly ungrammatical in Spanish, discrepancies between marginal dialects such as bozal and vestigial language and fluent Spanish are differences of degree. Nonetheless, a speaker who uses redundant subject pronouns upwards of 80% of the time, who uses coreferential subject pronouns two or more times in the same sentence, or who employs two or more noncoreferential 3rd person plural pronouns in the same sentence, would never be taken for a native speaker. Some examples from the present corpus illustrate the nonnative configurations that may be produced by vestigial speakers:

> *cuando ello hablo [ellos hablan], ello[s] comprenden*
>
> 'When they$_1$ speak, they$_2$ understand.' (TR)
>
> *yo comprendo y yo jablo*
> 'I understand and I speak.' (TR)
>
> *él tiene el cuatro y él juga [toca] y juga y él canta*
> 'He has a cuatro and he plays and he sings.' (TR)
>
> *elloh quieren el velso que ello jacen ahora*
> 'They$_1$ like the verses that they$_2$ are writing now.' (TR)
>
> *yo lo jablo onde yo quiero*
> 'I speak it wherever I want.' (PR)
>
> *yo tengo do sijo; yo tengo a Al y yo tengo a Paul*
> 'I have two sons, I have Al and I have Paul.' (IS)
>
> *cuando ella termina, ella tiene que tirá el agua*
> 'When she finishes, she has to throw out the water.' (IS)
>
> *ello[s] venden y ello[s] van*
> 'They sell and they go.' (CU)

cuando yo fui a Los Angeles, yo vi
'When I went to Los Angeles, I saw ...' (MX)

Yo les digo que yo enseño en Silliman
'I tell them that I teach in Silliman [University].' (PH)

Hispanic creole dialects normally employ subject pronouns obligatorily, due to the minimally inflected verbal systems; similar examples may be found in the Spanish of Equatorial Guinea, Chota, Ecuador, and bozal Spanish.

The vestigial Spanish dialects described above do not share all of the characteristics found among Afro-Iberian creoles, such as use of the second person singular subject pronoun *vos*, use of aspectual particles such as *ta*, massive neutralization of pronominal case and complete elimination of nominal inflection. On the positive side of the balance, several major areas have been delineated in which significant parallels are found between Afro-Hispanic creole and vestigial Spanish dialects deriving from demonstrably noncreole Spanish. Other cases of partial convergence could be added, including use of tener 'to have' as an existential verb, and phonological misidentification of word-initial and word-final consonants. It must be noted that the examples of creole-like structures found among vestigial Spanish speakers often represent a relatively small percentage of total usage; that is, grammatically acceptable utterances are produced alongside the examples cited above. It is not feasible to compute percentages of deviation from "standard" grammatical patterns among semispeakers, but the successive production of creolized and noncreolized forms by the same speakers is an index of the incomplete dominance of a consistent grammatical apparatus. Presumably, bozal/creole Spanish exhibited similar patterns in its later stages, as contact with large numbers of native speakers increased, and decreolization intensified. Partially decreolized contemporary dialects such as Colombian Palenquero, Zamboanga Chabacano, Panamanian Congo, the Chota Valley of Ecuador and even Papiamentu, exhibit similar alternation between earlier creole and modern Spanish forms. Since the only attestations of earlier Afro-Hispanic creoles are literary imitations, which stressed nonstandard forms while often paying no attention to the use of standard variants, it is not possible to know with certainty what percentage of noncreole forms were produced by Afro-Hispanic speakers at each successive stage of linguistic evolution.

The comparison of vestigial and creolized or post-creole Spanish dialects, as well as the noncreolized Spanish of Equatorial Guinea, leads to the conclusion that the conditions that have produced vestigial Spanish are parallel to those which led to earlier creolization (and are effectively the temporal inverse of the decreolization process), with the result that the similarities between vestigial and creole dialects are not fortuitous, but are rather a reflection of inherent evolutionary parallels. These conditions include the following:

(1) First generation creole speakers and vestigial language speakers are characterized by a lopsided competence/performance ratio, since their active abilities in the target language are far below their passive comprehension. Both groups, however, are capable of carrying out conversations in some form of the target language, and are thus a step above the passive bilingual.

(2) Both groups suffer from the lack of extensive contact with accurate native- speaker models, and do not develop the necessary self-monitoring feedback and correction mechanisms which eliminate certain deviations from widely accepted patterns among true native speakers. In the case of African slaves and servants in Spanish colonies, contact with native speakers of Spanish was usually limited to a few non-Africans, and in the case of plantation workers, who often interacted only with overseers of African descent, no contact with true native Spanish speakers may have been possible. Vestigial Spanish speakers typically are able to speak Spanish only with a tiny subset of their acquaintances, usually the oldest relatives or neighbors (many of whom may themselves exhibit reduced fluency in Spanish), and are not surrounded by an environment where Spanish in any form is spoken on a daily basis.

(3) As a consequence, both groups of speakers are forced to think partially or entirely in another language when speaking the target language (in this case Spanish), and their production in the latter language is characterized by considerable on-the-spot improvisation resulting in the high degree of heterogeneity among vestigial and pidgin/creole speakers.

(4) Neither bozal/creole nor vestigial Spanish speakers are under pressure to produce grammatically and/or socially acceptable Spanish; whether Spanish is spoken by choice or under protest, its use is purely pragmatic, and effective communication is valued more highly than grammatical precision. Both groups have arrived at approximations to received Spanish using similar linguistic strategies. No historical connection among the vestigial Spanish groups is necessary in order to account for the paths of evolution from fluent to vestigial Spanish in each area; it is enough to invoke natural and quasi-universal tendencies of imperfect learning. Reduction of phonological oppositions, conversion of variable phonological processes into categorical rules, preference for a single gender/number marker and for third-person (i.e., minimally marked) verbal forms, neutralization and elimination of prepositions in cases where general word order

permits extraction of meaning, avoidance of embedded structures and categorical use of subject pronouns, are all natural consequences of imperfect language acquisition under conditions where the need for essential communication prevails over pressures for normative precision.

The demonstration of linguistic parallels between bozal Spanish and vestigial Spanish derived from noncreole dialects does not in itself invalidate the postulate that a unified Afro-Hispanic creole with Portuguese roots was once widely spoken in Latin America and perhaps elsewhere. It does, however, weaken the force of arguments stressing the necessarily monogenetic origin of congruent grammatical structures among several creole dialects. Moreover, the preceding demonstrations stress the importance of the study of vestigial dialects and semispeakers in the context of historical linguistics and language creolization.

The preceding remarks have surveyed a number of contemporary Afro-Hispanic linguistic phenomena, as well as a set of speech phenomena reminiscent of Afro-Hispanic language but which stem from a significantly different set of parameters. The three possible counterexamples to unified monogenetic theories of Afro-Iberian creole formation have thus been given substance: (1) existence of Afro-Hispanic creoles significantly different from acknowledged Afro-Portuguese variants (Panamanian congo dialect and possibly Ecuadorian choteño); (2) Afro-Hispanic linguistic contacts which failed to produce configurations found in Afro-Iberian creoles (Equatorial Guinean Spanish); (3) the existence of archetypal Afro-Iberian creoloid structures in noncreole dialects in which the African/Portuguese element is absent (vestigial Spanish dialects). The results of the survey do not detract from the serious scholarship that has gone into demonstrating common structures and possibly common origins for many Iberian-based creoles; they do demonstrate, however, that a wider range of data must be taken into consideration before the book on creole formation can be closed. Such data can only come from the study of marginal, vestigial and isolated dialect pockets, most of which are little known and little studied, and many of which are rapidly disappearing. The search must go on.

REFERENCES

Alleyne, Mervyn. 1971. "The cultural matrix of creolization." *In Pidginization and Creolization of Languages*, ed. by Dell Hymes. Cambridge: Cambridge University, pp.169–86.

Allsopp, Richard. 1977. "La influencia africana sobre el idioma en el

Caribe." In *Africa en América Latina*, ed. by Manuel Moreno Fraginals. Mexico: Siglo XXI/UNESCO, pp.129–51.

Alvarez Nazario, Manuel. 1974. *El elemento afronegroide en el español de Puerto Rico.* San Juan: Instituto de Cultura Puertorriqueña.

Barrantes, D. V. 1882. *Recopilación en metro del bachiller Diego Sánchez de Badajoz.* Madrid: Librería de los Bibliófilos.

Bickerton, Derek. 1977. "Pidginization and creolization: language acquisition and language universals." In *Pidgin and Creole linguistics*, ed. by Albert Valdmann. Bloomington: Indiana University, pp. 49–69.

Bickerton, Derek and Aquiles Escalante. 1970. "Palenquero: a Spanish-based creole of northern Colombia." *Lingua* 32:254–67.

Birmingham, John. 1970. "The Papiamentu language of Curaçao." Ph.D. dissertation, University of Virginia.

Boretzky, Norbert. 1983. *Kreolsprachen Substratum und Sprachwandel.* Weisbaden: Otto Harrassowitz.

Bowen, J. Donald. 1971. "Hispanic languages and influence in Oceania." In *Current trends in linguistics*, vol. 8, ed. by Thomas Sebeok. The Hague: Mouton, pp. 938–52.

Canfield, D. Lincoln. 1981. *Spanish pronunciation in the Americas.* Chicago: University of Chicago.

Carriazo, J. 1954. "Negros, esclavos y extranjeros en el barrio sevillano de San Bernardo (1617–1629)." *Archivo Hispalense* 20(64–65):121–33.

Castellano, Juan. 1961. "El negro esclavo en el entremés del Siglo de Oro." *Hispania* 44:55–65.

Chasca, Edmund de. 1946. "The phonology of the speech of the negroes in early Spanish drama." *Hispanic Review* 14:322–39.

Chávez Franco, Modesto. 1930. *Crónicas del Guayaquil antiguo.* Guayaquil: Imp. y Talleres Municipales.

Coba Andrade, Carlos. 1980. *Literatura popular afroecuatoriana.* Otavalo: Instituto Otavaleño de Antropología.

Dorian, Nancy. 1977. "The problem of the semi-speaker in language death." *International Journal of the Sociology of Language* 12:23–32.

Drolet, Patricia. 1980. "The Congo ritual of northeastern Panama: an Afro-American expressive structure of cultural adaptation." Ph.D. dissertation, University of Illinois.

Escalante, Aquiles. 1954. "Notas sobre el Palenque de San Basilio, una comunidad negra en Colombia." *Divulgaciones Etnológicas* 3:207–359.

Estupiñán Tello, Julio. 1967. *El negro en Esmeraldas*. Quito: Casa de la Cultura Ecuatoriana.

Frake, Charles. 1971. "Lexical origins and semantic structure in Philippine creole Spanish." In *Pidginization and Creolization of Languages*, ed. by Dell Hymes. Cambridge: Cambridge University, pp. 223–42.

Franco Silva, Alfonso. 1979. *Registro documental sobre la esclavitud sevillana (1453–1513)*. Sevilla: Universidad de Sevilla.

Friedemann, Nina S. de and Carlos Patio Rosselli. 1983. *Lengua y sociedad en el Palenque de San Basilio*. Bogotá: Instituto Caro y Cuervo.

Góngora, Luis de. 1980. *Letrillas*. Critical ed. by Robert Jammes. Madrid: Clásicos Castalia.

González, Carlisle and Celso Benavides. 1982. "¿Existen rasgos criollos en el habla de Samaná?" In *El español del Caribe*, ed. by O. Alba, ed. Santiago de los Caballeros: Universidad Católica Madre y Maestra, pp. 105–32.

González Echegaray, Carlos. 1959. *Estudios guineos*: v. 1, filología. Madrid: Instituto de Estudios Africanos.

Granda, Germán de. 1968. "La tipología 'criolla' de dos hablas del área lingüística hispánica." *Thesaurus* 23:193–205.

———. 1969. "Posibles vías directas de introducción de africanismos en el 'habla de negro' literaria castellana." *Thesaurus* 24:459–69.

———. 1978. *Estudios lingüísticos hispánicos, afrohispánicos y criollos*. Madrid: Gredos.

———. 1984. "Perfil lingüístico de Guinea Ecuatorial." *Homenaje a Luis Flórez*, 1–77. Bogotá: Instituto Caro y Cuervo.

———. 1985. "Fenómenos de interferencia fonética de fang en el español de Guinea Ecuatorial." *Anuario de Lingüística Hispánica* 1:95–114 (Valladolid).

Guillotte, Joseph. 1982. *Masters of the marsh: an introduction to the ethnography of the Isleños of lower St. Bernard Parish, Louisiana*. New Orleans: University of New Orleans, Dept. of Geography and History.

Guy, Gregory. 1981. "Parallel variability in American dialects of Spanish and Portuguese." In *Variation omnibus* (NWAVE 8), ed. by D. Sankoff and H. Cedergren, Edmonton: Linguistic Research, pp. 85–96..

Hancock, Ian. 1975. "Malacca creole Portuguese: Asian, African or European?" *Anthropological Linguistics* 17:211–36.

Hymes, Dell, ed. 1971. *Pidginization and creolization of languages*. Cambridge: Cambridge University.

Jason, Howard. 1967. "The language of the negro in early Spanish drama." *College Language Association Journal* 10:330–40.

Joly, Luz Graciela. 1981. "The ritual play of the Congos of north-central Panama: its sociolinguistic implications." *Sociolinguistic Working Papers* no. 85 (Austin: Southwest Educational Development Laboratory).

Klumpp, Kathleen. 1970. "Black traders of north highland Ecuador." In *Afro-American anthropology: contemporary perspectives*, ed. by N. Whitten and J. Szwed, New York: Free Press, pp. 245–62.

Laurence, Kemlin. 1974. "Is Caribbean Spanish a case of decreolization?" *Orbis* 23:484–99.

Le Page, Robert. 1977. "Processes of pidginization and creolization." In *Pidgin and Creole linguistics*, ed. by Albert Valdmann. Bloomington: Indiana University, pp. 222–55.

Lipski, John. 1984. "Observations on the Spanish of Malabo, Equatorial Guinea: implications for Latin American Spanish." *Hispanic Linguistics* 1:69–96.

———. 1985a. *The Spanish of Equatorial Guinea*. Tübingen: Max Niemeyer.

———. 1985b. "The speech of the negros congos of Panama." *Hispanic Linguistics* 2(1):23–47.

———. 1985c. "Black Spanish: the last frontier of Afro-America." *Crítica* 1(2):53–75 (San Diego).

———. 1986. "A test case of the Afro-Hispanic connection: final /s/ in Equatorial Guinea." *Lingua* 68:357–70.

———. a. "On the construction tá + infinitive in bozal Spanish." *Romance Philology*, forthcoming.

———. b. "The reduction of /s/ in bozal Spanish." *Neophilologus*, forthcoming.

———. c. "El Valle del Chota: enclave lingüístico afroecuatoriano." *Boletín de la Academia Puertorriquena de la Lengua Española*, forthcoming.

———. d. "The impact of Louisiana isleño Spanish on historical dialectology." *Southwest Journal of Linguistics*, forthcoming.

———. e. "Creole Spanish and vestigial Spanish: evolutionary parallels." *Linguistics*, forthcoming.

———. f. "The Portuguese element in Philippine creole Spanish: a critical assessment." *Zeitschrift für romanische Philologie*, forthcoming.

———. g. "African Spanish phonetics: common traits and universal tendencies." *General Linguistics*, forthcoming.

———. h. "The Chota Valley: Afro-Hispanic language in highland Ecuador." *Latin American Research Review*, forthcoming.

Lope de Rueda. 1908. *Obras de Lope de Rueda*. Edition of the Real Academia Española. Madrid: Librería de los Sucesores de Hernando.

López Albújar, Enrique. 1966. *Matalaché*, 3rd ed. Lima: Editorial Juan Mejía.

MacCurdy, Raymond. 1950. *The Spanish dialect of St. Bernard Parish, Louisiana*. Albuquerque: University of New Mexico.

Mason, J. Alden and Aurelio Espinosa. 1927. "Porto Rican folklore: folktales." *Journal of American Folklore* 40:313–414.

Megenney, William. 1983. "La influencia del portugués en el palenquero colombiano." *Thesaurus* 38:548–63.

———. 1984. "Traces of Portuguese in three Caribbean creoles: evidence in support of the monogenetic theory." *Hispanic Linguistics* 1:177–89.

———. 1985. "La influencia criollo-portuguesa en el español caribeño." *Anuario de Lingüística Hispánica* (Valladolid) 1:157–80.

Meier, Guus and Pieter Muysken. 1977. "On the beginnings of pidgin and creole studies: Schuchardt and Hesseling." In *Pidgin and Creole linguistics*, ed. by Albert Valdmann. Bloomington: Indiana University, pp. 21–48.

Menéndez Pidal, Ramón. 1957. "Sevilla frente a Madrid." In *Estructuralismo e historia, miscelánea homenaje a André Martinet*, vol. 3, ed. by D. Catalán. La Laguna: Universidad de La Laguna, pp. 99–165.

Mintz, Sidney. 1971. "The socio-historical background to pidginization and creolization." In *Pidginization and Creolization of Languages*, ed. by Dell Hymes. Cambridge: Cambridge University, pp. 481–96.

Moodie, Sylvia. 1973. "The Spanish language as spoken in Trinidad." *Caribbean Studies* 13:88–94.

———. 1982. "Trinidad Spanish pronouns: a case of language death in the Caribbean." *Readings in Spanish-English contrastive linguistics*, III, Rose Nash, D. Belaval, eds., pp. 206–28. San Juan: Inter-American University.

———. a. "Morphophonemic illformedness in an obsolescent dialect: a case study of Trinidad Spanish." *Orbis*, forthcoming.

Naro, Anthony. 1978. "A study on the origins of pidginization." *Language* 54:314–47.

Otheguy, Ricardo. 1975. "The Spanish Caribbean: a creole perspective." In *New ways of analyzing variation in English*, Charles-James Bailey, Roger Shuy, eds., 323–39. Washington: Georgetown University.

Peñaherrera de Costales, Piedad and Alfredo Costales Samaniego. 1959. *Coangue o historia cultural y social de los negros del Chota y Salinas.* Quito: Llacta.

Perl, Matthias. 1982. "Creole morphosyntax in the Cuban 'habla bozal'." Studii si Cercetari Lingvistice 5:424–33.

———. a. "Die Bedeutung des Kreolenportugiesischen für ihre Herausbildung der Kreolensprachen in den Karibik." Unpublished MS, Karl-Marx Universität, Leipzig.

Pike, Ruth. 1967. "Sevillian society in the sixteenth century: slaves and freedmen." *Hispanic American Historical Review* 47:344–59.

Quilis, Antonio. 1980. "Le sort de l'espagnol aux Philippines: un problème de langues en contact." *Revue de Linguistique Romane* 44:82–107.

———. 1984. "La lengua española en las Islas Filipinas." *Cuadernos del Centro Cultural de la Embajada Española* (Manila) 11:1–22.

Reinecke, John. 1938. "Trade jargons and creole dialects as marginal languages." *Social Forces* 17:107–18.

Rout, Leslie. 1976. *The African experience in Spanish America*. Cambridge: Cambridge University.

Salvador Salvador, Francisco. 1978. *La neutralización l/r explosivas agrupadas y su área andaluza*. Granada: Universidad de Granada.

Sanders, A. C. 1982. *A social history of black slaves and freedmen in Portugal 1441–1555*. Cambridge: Cambridge University.

Sebeok, Thomas, ed. 1971. *Current trends in linguistics*, v. 8. The Hague: Mouton.

Sibayan, Bonifacio. 1971. "The Philippines." In *Current trends in linguistics*, vol. 8, ed. by Thomas Sebeok. The Hague: Mouton, pp. 1033–62.

Taylor, Douglas. 1971. "Grammatical and lexical affinities of creoles." *In Pidginization and Creolization of Languages*, ed. by Dell Hymes. Cambridge: Cambridge University, Hymes (1971: 293-6).

Thompson, Robert. 1957. "A preliminary survey of the Spanish dialect of Trinidad." *Orbis* 6:353-72.

Toscano Mateus, Humberto. 1953. *El español del Ecuador*. Madrid: Consejo Superior de Investigación Científica.

Trifonovitch, Gregory. 1971. "Trust territories of the Pacific Islands." In Current trends in linguistics, vol. 8, ed. by Thomas Sebeok. The Hague: Mouton, pp. 1063-87.

Valdmann, Albert, ed. 1977. *Pidgin and creole linguistics*. Bloomington: Indiana University.

Valkhoff, Marius. 1966. *Studies in Portuguese and Creole*. Johannesburg: Witwatersrand University.

Van Wijk, H. L. A. 1958. "Orígenes y evolución del papiamentu." *Neophilologus* 42:169-82.

Vila Vilar, Enriqueta. 1977. *Hispanoamérica y el comercio de esclavos: los asientos portugueses*. Sevilla: Escuela de Estudios Hispanoamericanos.

Weber de Kurlat, Frida. 1962. "Sobre el negro como tipo cómico en el teatro español del siglo XVI." *Romance Philology* 17:380-91.

Whinnom, Keith. 1954. "Spanish in the Philippines." *Journal of Oriental Studies* 1:129-94.

———. 1956. *Spanish contact vernaculars in the Philippines*. Hong Kong: Hong Kong University.

———. 1965. "Origin of European-based creoles and pidgins." *Orbis* 14:510-27.

Whitten, Norman. 1965. *Class, kinship and power in an Ecuadorian town: the negroes of San Lorenzo*. Stanford: Stanford University.

———. 1974. *Black frontiersmen: a South American case*. New York: John Wiley/Schenkman.

———, and Nina Friedemann. 1974. *La cultura negra del litoral ecuatoriano y colombiano: un modelo*. Bogotá: Instituto Colombiano de Antropología.

Wolf, Teodoro. 1892. *Geografía y geología del Ecuador*. Leipzig: F. A. Brockhaus.

Zárate, Manuel. 1962. *Socavón y tambor*. Panamá: Imprenta Nacional.

The Spanish Teacher as Dialectologist
Mark G. Goldin
George Mason University

Dialectology is rarely thought of as a branch of linguistics that offers applications for a teacher of standard languages. Yet particularly for a language like Spanish, spoken over a wide geographical area with well-documented variation, the methods of dialectology provide surprising insights into the process of language acquisition by classroom learners.

The question that occurs to most teachers in regard to Spanish dialects is whether the rigorous study of these varieties can suggest anything about which of the numerous varieties of the language should be taught in foreign language classrooms. While this issue is an interesting one, and while some answers to it may in fact be obtained from the formal study of dialects, it is far from the most important contribution of dialectology for the Spanish teacher. The question of the choice of a teaching dialect will be discussed later, but a more serious proposal is that knowledge of several approaches which have been used to describe and explain variation in Spanish is in the long run a much more useful tool for a Spanish teacher. These approaches combine to allow a teacher to examine the attempts of individual learners to speak or write in their new language. Learners' language contains a great amount of variation, and the methods of dialectology are therefore directly applicable to understanding the structure of learners' language.

Spanish dialects have been described from historical, structural, and quantitative viewpoints. Each of these approaches has developed insights into the process of language change and variation that can be used to examine the language of learners as well. In particular, the historical and quantitative approaches have a great deal to offer.

The historical approach to Spanish dialectology has attempted to provide explanations, usually in historical terms, for variation found in the contemporary language. For the study of American Spanish, this approach began when Rudolf Lenz traveled from Germany to Chile in the nineteenth century, and observed in the Spanish spoken in Chile differences from the language he was accustomed to hearing in Spain. In a paper published in 1893, Lenz ascribed the peculiarities of Chilean Spanish to a substratum based on the indigenous Araucanian language. According to Lenz, Chilean Spanish speakers who may never have heard the Araucanian language were using Spanish pronunciations influenced by it. Amado Alonso, in an article written in 1939, showed that Lenz's theory is inadequate to explain the nature of Chilean Spanish, since many of the same features found in Chilean occur in other areas of the Spanish-speaking world, including Spain itself, where there is no possibility of Araucanian-Spanish language contact (Alonso 1953). But the substratum theory of language variation is an attractive one; a more convincing presentation of substratum influence in contemporary Mexican Spanish is Lope Blanch (1967).

The question of Andalusian influence on American Spanish is a second contribution of historical dialectology. The similarity of the pronunciation of southern Spain to that of some regions of Spanish America has provoked a 60-year discussion of whether a causal relationship underlies this similarity (Henríquez Ureña 1921, 1925; Boyd-Bowman 1956; Guitart 1959; Danesi 1977). What matters here is that the historical approach to dialect variation should not be thought of as a throwback to nineteenth-century philology, but as an ongoing line of inquiry which continues to make serious contributions to knowledge of variation in Spanish.

The historical insight that promises most for second language teachers is wave theory, originally proposed by Schmidt (1872). Wave theory is the idea that new language forms travel through communities in waves, with one feature following another, until older forms have been replaced. A good statement of Schmidt's wave theory may be found in Pedersen (1931). While this model of language change comes from the Germanic linguistic tradition, it has been used to describe the history of Romance languages including Spanish (Malkiel 1983). Bailey (1973) was the first contemporary writer to use wave theory in describing language variation, but the clearest modern statement of how language forms spread in waves is presented by Wolfram and Fasold (1974). Their illustration (Figure 1) consists of a series of concentric ovals, each representing, in the original wave theory, a geographic area; but in the extended conception of the model, any community of speakers such as men or women, speakers of a particular age, or socioeconomic groups. The succession of ovals corresponds to the advance of time. The zeros, x's, and 1's found within each oval represent hypothetical linguistic features: a zero signifies the complete absence of a feature for a particular group of speakers; a 1 indicates that all the members of the group use the feature all the time; and an x means that the feature is used variably; that is, the same speakers sometimes do and at other times do not use the feature.

In the first small oval of Figure 1 (pg.76), one feature has begun to appear variably in one group of speakers; three other features have not yet appeared. By time iv, the first feature has become categorical in the first speaker group, while three more features have been introduced variably. The fourth feature has not yet appeared in any other group, but the first three occur variably in one or more of three additional communities. At time vii, all four features have replaced any former competitors in the original group; the first feature extends categorically to all four groups; and the three other features appear either variably or categorically in all four groups of speakers.

The notion of variability, the idea that a single speaker uses sometimes one, sometimes another form for the same meaning, is the primary link between wave theory and second language learning. After examining some other approaches to dialectology, we shall consider how the wave model combines with other insights to provide a way of observing and anticipating the behavior of second-language learners.

Structural dialectology approaches language variation from a different perspective. While historical dialectology is concerned with the causes of variation and change, structural dialectologists asked about the effect of new forms on the system underlying the observed forms. For example, Hyman (1956), observing the occurrence of the velar nasal in word-final position in several Spanish dialects, decided to analyze the almost-minimal pair *conejo ~ con eso* [konexo ~ koŋ eso] by postulating an open juncture phoneme / + / whose occurrence conditioned the velar nasal in *con eso*. In her view, the existence of the velar nasal in some dialects indicated a phonological unit of juncture, different from the velar nasal itself. By contrast, working within the same approach, Honsa (1965) reached a different solution to a similar dialect problem. In observing the pronunciation of *s* as [h] in preconsonantal and word-final position in Argentine Spanish, Honsa concluded that this phenomenon indicated the existence of a new phoneme /h/ that does not occur in dialects without *s ~h* alternation. He analyzed the minimal pair *es Argentina ~ esa Argentina* [eharxentina ~ esarxentina] as instances of the contrasting phonemes /h/ and /s/. Of course, these analysts' unwillingness to propose that word boundaries affect pronunciation is what led to their defining these data as thorny problems in the first place. These examples of the structural approach illustrate the structuralists' interest in an underlying linguistic system apart from the observed forms themselves.

Although there is no direct application of the structuralist approach for teaching second languages, the approach is important because it led to a third way of looking at dialect variation, a quantitative approach which can combine with the historical perspective in asking not only why speech forms vary, but also what type of system underlies variable speech.

Quantitative dialectology has evolved in large measure from Labov's early work on English (Labov 1966). This approach takes the position that there is

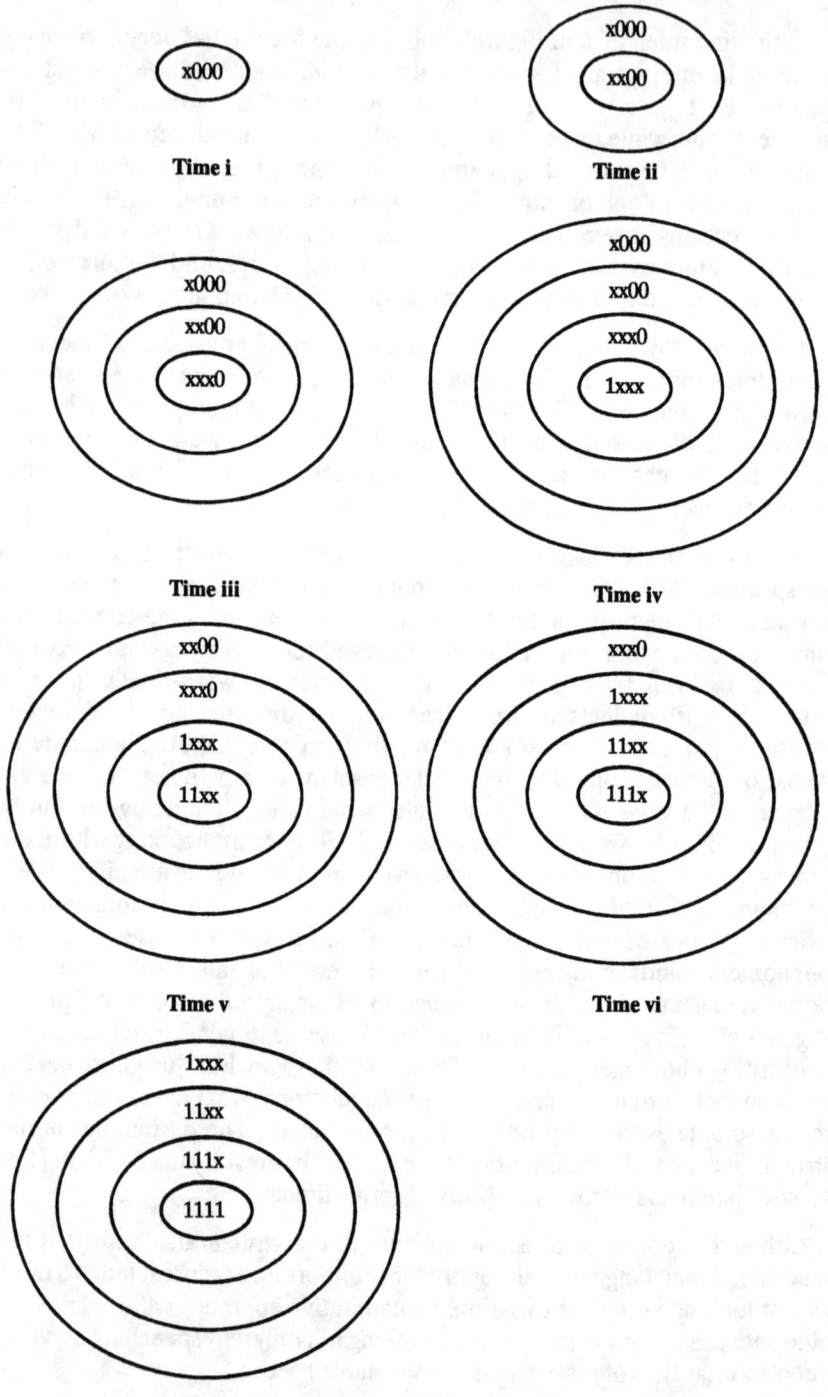

Fig. 1. Wave spread (from Wolfram and Fasold 1974:76)

rarely such a thing as free variation, and that when a single speaker uses now one form, now another in what appears to be the same environment, there is almost always a systematic factor governing the occurrence of one or another form. Ma and Herasimchuk (1971), Fontanella de Weinberg (1973), and Perissinotto (1975) are classic examples of the quantitative approach to Spanish dialectology. These investigators counted the occurrence of variable pronunciations, correlated the occurrences with sex, age, social class, and contextual style; and found convincing evidence that an underlying system shared by members of each particular community determines the frequency with which they use variable forms in particular contexts. Speakers who omit final *s*, for example, do so much more often when speaking informally than when speaking or reading aloud in situations where attention may be focused on the form of their speech. Upper-class speakers and women often, though not always, demonstrate more attention to the form of their speech. Such observations make clear that when two or more forms are used variably, each has a relative prestige within the community that accounts for the frequency with which it occurs in particular situations. Speakers' unconscious awareness of the social values of competing forms is as systematic as their knowledge of invariable language forms. At the same time, changing prestige is shown to be the cause of changes in the pattern of variation within a community, of the spread of forms through communities, and of the disappearance of one or more variable forms in cases where a single form prevails and becomes categorical.

The quantitative study of variable nonstandard dialect forms has made clear that speakers typically know and use both standard and nonstandard (prestigious and stigmatized) forms. The prestigious forms appear most often—though not necessarily with extremely high frequency—in formal contexts where a speaker pays more attention to form, and least often in informal contexts where a speaker focuses on meaning.

A language type which has been profitably studied through the quantitative approach is the creole language. Creole languages are of special interest to second-language teachers, because creoles exist in situations that most closely parallel the language learning situation. These languages have evolved in situations of contact between speakers of different languages where one community was socially greatly superior to the other—typically situations of slavery or colonial domination. Creoles are ordinarily spoken in communities where a standard language is also known and used to some extent by creole speakers. Certain creole speakers know the standard language well, and use features of it in even their most informal creole speech. Other speakers know the standard language less well, and use creole features when they try to speak the standard, while their informal speech is more "purely" creole.

The best-known Spanish-based creole is Palenquero, which is spoken in a black community in coastal Colombia. Palenquero has been described by

Montes (1962), Bickerton and Escalante (1970), Friedemann and Patiño (1983), and Megenny (1986). The Palenquero examples shown below are from Lewis (1974).

Palenquero personal pronouns include first person singular *i*, first person plural *suto* (from *nosotros*), and second person *bo* (from *vos*). As is typical of creole languages, Palenquero verbs have no endings for person, number, and tense; rather, verbs are accompanied by aspectual particles not found in standard Spanish. Some Palenquero aspectual particles are the perfective *a* (probably from Spanish *ha*), progressive *ba* (from *va*), imperfective *ta* (probably from *está*), and habitual *ase* (from *hace*). Some pure Palenquero forms using these forms, plus other words of obvious Spanish origin, are:

suto a sali 'we left'

bo a sabe 'you knew'

suto ta ba baila 'we were dancing'

i ta ba kanda 'I was singing'

i ase trabaha 'I work'

ele ase bebe 'he drinks'

Speakers use creole forms like these in combination with other forms that are closer to standard Spanish, as in the following examples:

suto bamos 'we are going'

i ase trabaha i ayulo mailo mi 'I work and help my husband'

anoche i ta ba kandando 'last night I was singing'

Forms like *bamos, ayulo,* and *kandando* manifest standard Spanish morphology which is not part of the pure creole system. Yet in the latter two examples, Spanish forms are used next to creole aspectual particles, showing how the same speakers mix creole and standard forms. The standard forms occur in formal situations where the speaker needs or wishes to cause a good impression linguistically. Quantitative studies of creole communities search for the factors that condition the mix of pure creole with standard forms.

Creole studies are relevant to second language teachers, because the language of an individual who is in the process of acquiring a new language is not unlike that of a creole speaker in the position of trying to use the more prestigious language forms in his repertoire. The learner communicates with partial knowledge of a standard language, whose forms are used accurately when circumstances permit their recall. Inaccurate forms of the new language occur when the learner's attention is focused less on the form and more on meaning.

Having viewed the historical, structural, and quantitative approaches to dialectology, it is possible to return to the two questions posed at the outset: Which varieties are most appropriate for classroom learning, and how can the methods of dialectology be applied to the analysis of learners' language? The first question is the more frequently asked, but the less interesting from the standpoint of dialectology, for only one of the criteria for choosing a classroom dialect has been illuminated by dialect research. That is the criterion of prestige, according to which, all other things being equal, a socially more prestigious form is preferred to a less prestigious one. The other criteria are frequency, that is, the likelihood of a learner encountering a speaker of a particular variety; and a more problematic criterion, ease of acquisition, according to which a variety that is easier to acquire is preferred to one that is more difficult. Unfortunately, there is no way of knowing a priori which of two competing forms is easier to acquire. However, for the purpose of exemplifying how the criteria for dialect choice work together, it is assumed that a system with fewer contrasting forms is easier to acquire than a system with more forms.

Consider the various systems of pronouns of address that are used in Spanish. System A has the most users in the Spanish-speaking world; contains as few forms as any of the others, or fewer; and, in the regions where the

singular		plural
	System A	
tú (familiar)		*ustedes*
usted (polite)		
	System B	
tú (familiar)		*vosotros* (familiar)
usted (polite)		*ustedes* (polite)
	System C	
vos (familiar)		*ustedes*
usted (polite)		
	System D	
vos (familiar)		*ustedes*
tú (polite)		
usted (ultrapolite)		

Fig. 2. Spanish pronouns of address

system is found, it is used by the most prestigious speakers. Not surprisingly, then, system A is the system of pronouns of address most commonly presented to nonnative speakers in textbooks and classrooms. Where system A is not chosen as a classroom dialect, the criterion of prestige can be seen to predominate; since system B is quite frequently taught in Spanish classes and textbooks even though it is more difficult than either system A or C by virtue of having one additional form. Also, while system B has fewer native speakers than system A, it also has fewer than system C, which is used in several regions while B occurs only in Spain. System B is universally prestigious in the Hispanic world, a fact which makes it a candidate for selection as a teaching dialect. System C lacks this universal prestige, and despite its frequency is almost never taught to foreigners. System D, which is used in parts of Central America, has the least prestige, the fewest speakers, and the most forms, thus meeting none of the criteria for choice as an appropriate variety for foreigners.

A more interesting pedagogical dilemma is posed by the choice of a system of clitic object pronouns. Systems W and X are the two which enjoy prestige in the Hispanic world. System X, which is standard in much of Spain, is somewhat more complex than W, which is standard in most of Latin America, but this fact does not prevent it from being chosen as worth presenting to foreigners. A competing system which is simpler, but lacks prestige, is system Y, which has been known and condemned in Spain for years, but may actually be gaining in frequency (Klein 1981), since it partially omits the distinction between direct and indirect object. That distinction is notoriously thorny for nonnatives, so system Z, which eliminates the distinction entirely, has been proposed as a system that can be helpful to foreigners although it is not used by native speakers anywhere in the Hispanic world (Goldin 1983). Another advantage of Z is that a user of it would not be stigmatized in the same way as a user of Y. Of course, Z is appropriate only for beginning learners as a way to use object pronouns for communication early in the acquisition process. It is to be expected that an advanced learner will eventually acquire one of the systems that are actually used by native speakers, without formal instruction in its complexities.

As interesting as the question of dialect choice may be, it is only tangentially related to dialect research. Much more central is the analysis of learners' communicative efforts, since this type of language is a highly variable system which can be analyzed according to the methods of dialectology. The beginning of this line of inquiry has appeared in a new book by Adamson (1987), as well as in the work of Zobl (1984). These investigators have observed that learners' language has properties which are parallel to those of nonstandard native dialects, including creole varieties.

Specifically, learners' language varies such that the most nearly standard or accurate forms occur in contexts where the learner has the greatest oppor-

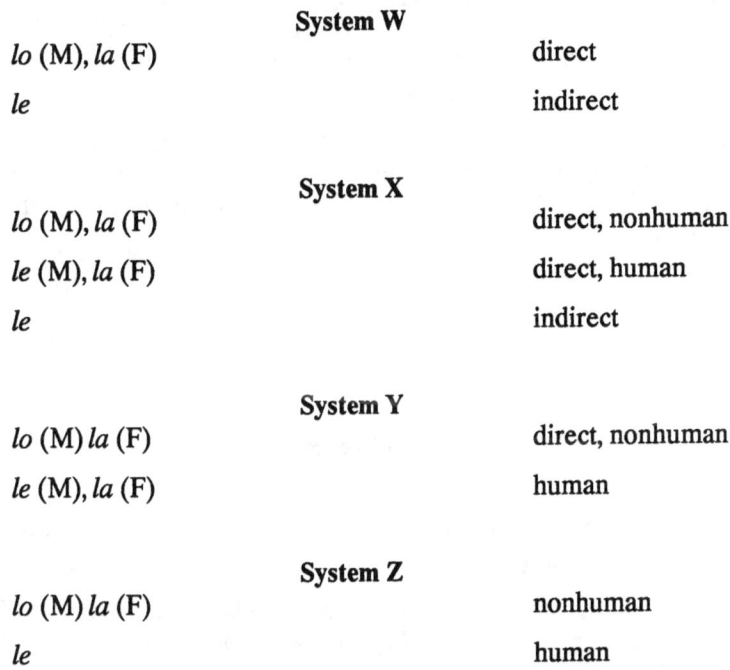

Fig. 3. Spanish object pronouns

tunity to monitor his language, such as reading aloud, reciting memorized passages, or completing drills and discrete-point exercises. The standard forms that a learner is able to produce in these monitored contexts appear less frequently in ordinary free writing and natural speech, just as variable forms used by native speakers occur less frequently in informal contexts.

Dialectology offers important implications for a second-language teacher, then, particularly in regard to the evaluation of learners' development. Assuming that the goal is for learners to use standard forms in the same situations where native speakers use them, it is not enough to evaluate students' performance exclusively in formal situations like reading aloud, filling in blanks, or choosing the correct form. Ability to succeed in this type of testing situation does not mean that accurate forms will also be used in less formal contexts in which there is a desired communicative outcome apart from correctness of language. On the other hand, the accurate use of standard forms in real-life conversation and free writing probably does imply the use of standard forms in monitored situations.

This does not mean that there is no place for tests involving highly monitored situations. If, as is usual, a learner does not use standard "correct" forms in natural situations, it is informative to determine whether accurate forms occur in monitored contexts. It is important to realize that no evidence suggests that natural development progresses from monitored to informal contexts. Rather, the presence of accurate forms only in monitored contexts can be taken as indication that although the form or rule may have been learned, acquisition still needs to take place.

Research on variability in learners' language can be expected to contribute in the years ahead to understanding of how second language acquisition develops. It is clear that the methods of dialectology have an important part in this task.

References

Adamson, H. D. 1987. *Variation theory and second language acquisition.* Washington: Georgetown University Press.

Alonso, Amado. 1953. "Examen de la teoría indigenista de Rodolfo Lenz." In *Estudios lingüísticos, temas hispanoamericanos*, by Amado Alonso, pp. 332–398. Madrid: Gredos.

Bailey, Charles-James N. 1973. *Variation and linguistic theory.* Washington: Georgetown University Press.

Bickerton, Derek and Aquiles Escalante. 1970. "Palenquero: A Spanish-based creole of northern Colombia." *Lingua* 24:254–67.

Boyd-Bowman, Peter. 1956. "The regional origins of the earliest Spanish colonists of America." *PMLA* 80:1152–72.

Danesi, Marcel. 1977. "The case for andalucismo revisited." *Hispanic Review* 45:191–193.

Fontanella de Weinberg, María Beatriz. 1973. "Comportamiento ante -s de hablantes masculinos y femeninos del español bonaerense." *Romance Philology* 27:50–58.

Friedemann, Nina S. and Carlos Patiño Rosselli. 1983. *Lengua y sociedad en El Palenque de San Basilio.* Bogotá: Instituto Caro y Cuervo.

Goldin, Mark G. 1983. "Spanish clitics in the learner's dialect." In *Spanish and Portuguese in social context*, ed. by John J. Bergen and Garland D. Bills, pp. 55–60. Washington: Georgetown University Press.

Guitart, Guillermo. 1959. "Cuervo, Henríquez Ureña y la polémica del andalucismo en América." *Thesaurus* 14:20–81.

Henríquez Ureña, Pedro. 1921. "Observaciones sobre el español de América." *Revista de Filología Española* 7:357–90.

———. 1925. "El supuesto andalucismo de América." *Cuadernos del Instituto de Filología* 2:114–22.

Honsa, Vladimir. 1965. "The phonemic systems of Argentinian Spanish." *Hispania* 48:275–83.

Hyman, Ruth L. 1956. "[+] as an allophone denoting open juncture in several Spanish-American dialects." *Hispania* 39:293–99.

Klein, Flora. 1981. "Neutrality, or the semantics of gender in a dialect of Castilla." In *Linguistic symposium on Romance languages*: 9, ed. by William W. Cressey and Donna Jo Napoli, pp. 164–76. Washington: Georgetown University Press.

Labov, William 1966. *The social stratification of English in New York City*. Washington: Center for Applied Linguistics.

Lenz, Rudolf. 1893. "Beitrage zur Kenntnis des Amerikanospanischen." *Zeitschrift für Romanische Philologie* 17:188–214. Spanish version: "Para el conocimiento del español de América." In *Estudios chilenos* (Biblioteca de dialectología hispanoamericana, 6). Buenos Aires: Instituto de Filología, 1940.

Lewis, Anthony. 1974. "San Basilio de Palenque—A 'post-creole' community?" Paper presented at the winter meeting of the Linguistic Society of America.

Lope Blanch, Juan M. 1967. "La influencia del sustrato en la fonética del español de México." *Revista de Filología Española* 50:145–61.

Ma, Roxana and Eleanor Herasimchuk. 1971. "The stylistic structure of Puerto Rican Spanish phonological variables." In *Bilingualism in the barrio*, ed. by Joshua Fishman, pp. 375–90. Bloomington: Indiana University.

Malkiel, Yakov. 1983. "Alternatives to the classic dichotomy 'Family tree/wave theory?': The Romance evidence." In *Language change*, ed. by Irmengard Rauch and Gerald F. Carr, pp. 192–256. Bloomington: Indiana University Press.

Megenney, William. 1986. *El palenquero: un lenguaje post-criollo de Colombia*. Bogotá: Instituto Caro y Cuervo.

Montes, José J. 1962. "Sobre el habla de San Basilio de Palenque." *Thesaurus* 17:446–50.

Pedersen, Holger. 1931. *The discovery of language: Linguistic science in the nineteenth century.* Bloomington: Indiana University Press.

Perissinotto, Giorgio. 1975. *Fonología del español hablado en la Ciudad de México.* Mexico City: El Colegio de México.

Schmidt, Johannes. 1872. *Die Verwandtschaftsverhältnisse der indogermanischen Sprachen.* Weimar: Hermann Böhlau.

Wolfram, Walt, and Ralph W. Fasold. 1974. *The study of social dialects in American English.* Englewood Cliffs, NJ: Prentice-Hall.

Zobl, Helmut. 1984. "The wave model of linguistic change and the naturalness of interlanguage." *Studies in Second Language Acquisition* 6:160–85.

Noun Gender Categories in Spanish and French: Form-Based Analyses and Comparisons

Richard V. Teschner

University of Texas at El Paso

The gender of roughly 96% of all [–HUMAN] nouns in Spanish can be determined by just four rules. These rules, together with supporting evidence which is expanded upon for the first time in the present paper, were initially set forth in Teschner and Russell (1984). The rules are these, and are to be applied in the order in which they are listed:

1) Nouns ending in *a* or *d* are overwhelmingly feminine. (Throughout this paper I will use "overwhelming" or "overwhelmingly" as technical terms to mean "90–100% conformity to rule/type.")

2) Nouns ending in *n, z* or *s* are moot, i.e., indeterminate as to gender. (Again "moot" and "indeterminate as to gender" are to be taken as technical terms meaning "less than 70% conformity to rule/type.")

3) However, nouns ending in *n* can be profitably subcategorized thereby revealing two groupings that are easy to remember with the aid of a mnemonic device:

   (i) Nouns ending in *ión* whose pre-antepenultimate letter is *c, g, n, s, t,* or *x* ("cig 'n' stix" or "cigarette and sticks") are overwhelmingly — indeed almost unanimously — feminine, as are a large number of nouns which end in *azón*.

   (ii) All other nouns which end in *n* are overwhelmingly masculine.

4) Overwhelmingly masculine are all other word-final endings. They are, in descending order of frequency of occurrence: *o, e, r, l, i, u, y, t, m, x,* plus the nine remaining Spanish alphabet graphemes or digraphs which can appear in noun-final position, each of which has fewer than 30 examples

in the lexicon: *b, c, ch, f, g, j, k, ll,* and *p.* (No Spanish nouns end in *h, ñ, q, rr, v* or *w.*)

Further study reveals that nouns ending in *s* can be subcategorized as well, though less economically than *n* nouns: those ending in *sis* or *tis* referring (as almost all do) to medical phenomena are overwhelmingly feminine, while compound nouns (almost always consisting of verb + noun, e.g., *el paracaídas*) are overwhelmingly masculine, and noncompound nouns excluding those that end in *sis* or *tis* are largely masculine (here "largely" is also a technical term meaning "70–89.9% conformity to rule/type"). Nouns that end in *z* do not lend themselves well to any sort of subcategorization; the closest one can get to "overwhelming" status is the subcategory *ez*, just 84.21% of whose constituents are feminine, though semantic considerations aid us in remembering which ones they are: feminine *ez* nouns denote abstract qualities, thus *la estrechez* "narrowness," *la rigidez* "rigidity," while masculine *ez* nouns do not (examples: *el ajedrez* "chess," *el jerez* "sherry"). There are 80 nouns ending in *iz*. Exactly half are feminine and half are masculine, and the only grounds – formal or functional – upon which to base any sort of a distinction are those that require us once again to take the last four letters of words into account: all nouns which end in *briz, driz* or *triz* are feminine. Nouns ending in *az* or *uz* are largely masculine, while nouns that end in *oz*, the smallest of the five second-letter-from-the-end subcategories, are essentially indeterminate as to gender.

The statistics on which these conclusions are based, and which are presented in considerable detail in Teschner and Russell (1984), were compiled from an unpublished inverse Spanish dictionary that processed the contents of the 18th edition of the Royal Academy dictionary (*El diccionario de la lengua española,* 1956). Throughout the 1960s and early 1970s, the late Prof. Russell was at work on this inverse dictionary, unfortunately never published because the Stahl and Scavnicky (1973) reverse dictionary of Spanish was printed first. Increasing ill health forced postponement of various studies that Prof. Russell had intended to base on his material. Unlike Stahl and Scavnicky (1973), Prof. Russell listed noun genders, distinguished transitivity among verbs, and provided part-of-speech labels for all other entries. I should add that with Prof. Russell's death in December of 1984, nascent plans to prepare his corpus for publication were once again abandoned; other factors having weight in the decision not to carry on the project were the proximate appearance of the 20th edition of the Royal Academy dictionary (1985) and the news of the completion of the as-yet-unpublished *Diccionario inverso de la lengua española* (Faitelson-Weiser 1985), which is based on 17 lexicographical sources in addition to the Royal Academy dictionary and whose more than 160,000 individual entries far exceed the approximately 89,000 which the 18th (1956) edition of the Royal Academy work contains.

The Teschner/Russell paper was written in large part as a response to the work of Bergen (1978), which summed up most previous studies on Spanish gender and constituted the best work on the topic at the time. Unlike Bergen 1978 and other corpus-based analyses (see for example Bull 1965, Doman 1982), Teschner and Russell 1984 employs the lengthiest dictionary in Spanish as its corpus; the other works employed far smaller corpora. Teschner and Russell limits its statistical presentation and subsequent conclusions to phonological rules of noun gender as opposed to semantic rules. Regarding assignment of gender via the application of semantic rules, the following principles govern: a noun referring to one male human is almost always masculine and a noun referring to one female human is almost always feminine. (Examples that are rule conforming include: *el cocinero/la cocinera, el hombre/la mujer, el siquiatra/la siquiatra* — the last pair belonging to that category of nouns known as "gender ambivalent" or "common gender" which is characterized by nouns whose forms do not inflect for gender, whose semantic content does not reveal the gender of its *signifié*, and whose gender reference can only be determined from modifiers such as articles, demonstratives, adjectives and the like.) Exceptions to "natural-gender" rules in Spanish are the so-called "epicene" nouns like *persona* and *víctima* whose gender as well as whose form remain constant — that is, feminine — regardless of the sex of the referent (thus *Este señor es una persona magnífica/Esta señora es una persona magnífica*).

From Appendix A, a summation of the statistics and the analysis in Teschner and Russell (1984), the following additional conclusions can be drawn about [−HUMAN] noun gender in Spanish:

(1) The old first-year textbook equating word-final *a* nouns with feminine gender and *o* nouns with masculine — and effectively consigning those nouns which end in some other letter to morphological limbo — is still a good way to begin one's study of the Spanish noun-gender system, since as 15,991 nouns end in *a* and 12,552 in *o*, their combined total of 28,543 equals 68.15% — slightly more than two-thirds — of the number of nouns in the entire corpus (41,882).

(2) The importance of arriving at a subcategorization of the otherwise indeterminate-as-to-gender *n* noun category is underscored by its position as third largest, with 4,404 entries. It will be noted that the present paper's subcategorization of feminine *-n* nouns as "cgnstx + *ión* and *azón*" contrasts markedly with the way this topic is handled by all other authors, who divide *n* nouns into "all *ión* as feminine" on the one hand, "the remainder as masculine" on the other. Such a classification has one disadvantage in that, by not excluding masculine nouns like *el rabión, el meridión, el camión, el sarampión, el embrión, el gorrión, el guión, el aluvión, el avión*, etc., it expands the number of exceptions to the rule. However, even with the inclusion of other types of *ión* nouns the number of masculine exceptions remains

small—about four dozen of a total 2,201—and in the long run the decision as to what to include or throw out will hinge on whether ease of learning or descriptive power is the prime consideration.

(3) Nouns ending in *e, r* and *l* constitute the fourth-, fifth-, and sixth-largest categories respectively, with *e* nouns representing 3,006 or 7.18%, *r* nouns 1,448 or 3.46%, and *l* nouns 1,165 or 2.78% of the total corpus. The *r* and *l* nouns share a trait that *e* nouns do not—at 98.55% and 97.85% conformity to type, respectively, they are almost as masculine-gender dominant as *o* nouns at 99.87% and more in conformity to type than *a* nouns at 96.30%. The *e* nouns by contrast do not technically qualify as "overwhelming" in conformity since with 89.35% of items masculine and 10.65% feminine, masculine predominance falls just short of the 90% minimum I have established as the cut-off. Yet when placed in the wider context of the remaining 23 noun-final gender groupings, *e* nouns are seen as the lowest in the series of upper-level percentages that form a continuum from *o* (99.89% conformity) through *t* (92.86%), *x* (90.91%) and finally *e* (89.35% conformity, as noted); the continuum ceases at this point, since the next highest percentage of conformity to type are *z* nouns at 61.63% feminine predominant. Thus a full 27.72 percentage points intervene between *e*'s 89.35 and *z*'s 61.63.

Various linguists have sought to establish a relationship between form and frequency of usage and the status of many *e* nouns as feminine. Thus Bergen (1978:872): "Nouns of high frequency with a stressed *á*- in the first syllable are generally feminine." To examine this assumption, Teschner and Russell (1984:126-8) compiled a list of all *e* nouns that contained a stressed /a/ in the initial syllable. While the details of the investigation need not be recapitulated here, the general conclusions bear repeating: since at no time do feminine *e* nouns achieve even majority status in either of the categories stipulated ("high frequency," "initial syllable tonic *a*") or in a combination thereof, "the relationship between first-syllable tonic /a/-stressed nouns and the feminine gender is suggestive (especially when dealing with high-frequency items)" but hardly categorical (Teschner and Russell 1984:127). Similarly, no other large-scale subcategorization scheme was found useful in relating *e* nouns to feminine gender, though two small subcategories—post-tonic C(onsonant) + *ie* (e.g., *la especie, la efigie*) excluding nouns ending in *pie* (e.g., *el traspié*), and *umbre* nouns, with 20 and 36 constituents respectively—are not without a certain limited utility, although in the end one is forced to the conclusion that most feminine *e* nouns must simply be memorized for gender, as "exceptions to the rule" that cannot be profitably explained by subcategorization.

Useful though these various statistics are, their utility can be further enhanced by viewing them through a wider-angled lens designed to encompass their totality, with one eye cocked toward comparing them with similar statistics from French, which will be presented later on in this paper. Here are some facts: slightly more than half (52.55% = 22,011 of 41,882) of all [−HUMAN] Spanish nouns are masculine, leaving 47.45% = 19,871 as feminine. It is facts like these, combined with the total number of categories (19) that are overwhelmingly masculine vs. the two that are overwhelmingly feminine, in addition to various considerations either semantic or pronominal, that lead us to conclude that of the two genders, feminine is marked and masculine unmarked. Other facts: 35,942 [−HUMAN] nouns (=17,059 + 18,883) belong to categories that are either overwhelmingly feminine dominant (*a, d*) or overwhelmingly masculine dominant (*l, o, r, e* et al.) respectively. These 35,942 represent 85.82% of the total corpus of 41,882 nouns. If we add to that total the 4,404 *n* nouns—and we recall that the *n* category nicely lends itself to subcategorization as half masculine and half feminine—then 40,346 or 96.33% of all the nouns in our corpus belong to categories that are overwhelmingly one gender or the other. By further refining our analysis to include only those individual nouns—not whole categories—which conform to the equivalency rule in question, i.e., only the 309 masculine *i* nouns and not the 23 *i* nouns which, as feminine, are exceptions to the rule, we arrive at the following figures: in Spanish, 40,305 i.e., 96.23% (16,642 + 2,273 = 18,715 + 20,590 which is the sum of 2,131 and 18,459) of all [−HUMAN] nouns are non-exception-forming rule-governed members of a small number of categories (*a/d* = fem.; *n* = fem. if *ión/azón*, *n* = masc. if "other"; all other terminal letters = m. if not *z* or *s*) whose rules are easy to conceptualize and even easier to remember. Note the very small (.10%) difference between the whole-category percentages and the rule-conforming-item-only percentages.

In sum, slightly more than 19 of every 20 Spanish nouns should be easy to master for gender. Spanish, then, is a "gender-simple" language.

If Spanish is a "gender-simple" language then French can be called a "gender-difficult" language. This fact has been commented on, at times to the point of exaggeration, by generations of scholars in a multitude of lands. Thus Goodluck (1831:2) refers to noun gender as "the greatest obstacle to the acquirement of the French language." For Ayer (1885:168) a knowledge of Latin etyma is the only key to success in mastering French noun gender ("... *la détermination par la forme ne peut se faire qu'en recourant à la source de la langue, au latin*"), a point of view taken to its logical, extreme atomistic conclusion 72 years later by Keys (1957:3), for whom

> ... the whole conception of ascribing one gender or the other to groups or words with any particular ending is fundamentally unsound, unless the ending can be explained historically and etymologically. ... Here is a case, if ever there was one, for eschewing overgeneralizing and for proclaiming once again the imperative principle: *chaque mot a son histoire*.

During the heyday of the audio-lingual movement, the French-American linguist Albert Valdman (1961:59) was to take a similarly radical position with regard to French noun gender:

> French nouns are arbitrarily assigned to one of two classes traditionally called masculine and feminine. By arbitrary we simply mean that the membership of a particular noun to [sic] one or the other of the two classes is not determined by any specific factor: phonemic shape, spelling, etymology or meaning.

While large numbers of French grammars have attempted to correlate gender with Latin noun classes, written endings, and semantic characteristics, for Valdman "... such formulations must be accompanied by long lists of exceptions which the learner must memorize." In the finest traditions of the pattern drill, Valdman finds that "a more efficient and linguistically sound method consists of substitution of nouns in noun phrases" (Valdman 1961:59), a stance supported in 1964 by Chevalier et al. (1964:164) (*"La forme du substantif ne permet pas de reconnaître le genre auquel il appartient ... C'est l'accord de l'article ou des adjectifs déterminatifs qui révèle le genre du substantif"*). It should be noted that by 1976 Valdman had modified his stance somewhat in light of the watershed work of Richard Tucker and associates, publication of which was begun in the late 1960s; in his *Introduction to French Phonology and Morphology* (Valdman 1976:146), he admits that "French speakers assign gender, at least in part, on the basis of the phonological form of nouns."

Beginning with the publication of "A Psychological Investigation of French Speakers' Skill with Grammatical Gender" (Tucker et al. 1968), Tucker and his McGill University colleagues André Rigault and Wallace Lambert were to publish a series of reports, culminating in the seminal Tucker et al. 1977 whose appendices we will examine in detail toward the end of the present paper, which increasingly burnt off a good amount of the fog that had previously shrouded the relationship between form and noun gender in French; yet Tucker et al. themselves admit that (1968:312)

> ... the mastery of gender is perhaps the most difficult and frustrating feature of the study of French as a second language, especially for those whose native language lacks gender distinctions.

In ignorance of Tucker's work or despite it, subsequent commentators continued to stress the anarchy and the difficulty of the French noun gender system; thus the highly prestigious Maurice Grevisse (1980:265), in the eleventh edition of his widely consulted reference grammar *Le bon usage*, again retained his widely quoted judgment to the effect that

> *Ce n'est guère que par l'usage que l'on apprend à reconnaître le genre des noms. Il y a cependant, pour les noms de choses, quelques règles générales qui, en dépit des exceptions qu'elles comportent, peuvent fornir des indications utiles.*

According to the statistics which I have compiled from Tucker et al., as supplemented by my compilations from Quemada (1966), roughly 73% of all French nouns belong to categories characterized by "overwhelming" conformity to rule. The 73% figure demonstrates two things: (1) that claims as to the anarchy and incoherence of French noun gender as voiced by grammarians from Goodluck through Grevisse were exaggerated, but (2) when compared to the "gender-simple" Spanish noun gender system, French noun gender is indeed "difficult" in that it lends itself far less well to description. This lack of descriptive ease is greatly compounded when we learn that about two dozen separate categories are needed to adequately classify the gender patterns of French nouns. (Again, more on this below.)

As a Romance language, French is necessarily cognate to a greater or lesser degree with all other Romance languages; thus a good working knowledge of another Romance language can be assumed to stand learners of French in good stead when they study it. The question then becomes, How good a stead?

Romance philologists have long known that of all the Latin-derived languages, French has evolved the furthest from the parent Latin. Compared with French, the other Romance tongues are conservative. Posner (1966:133) for example notes that "there are signs that the gender system is not as vigorous [in French] as elsewhere in Romance. It may even be that its survival into modern times owes a great deal to the pressures exercised by conservative factors." In his study of forms and degrees of recognizability among Romance cognates, Richman (1970) not surprisingly reports that the distance between French on the one hand and Italian, Spanish or Portuguese on the other is greater than the distance between any combination of these last three languages: "French appears to be the most deviant of the four languages, showing up in only the three lowest percentages" (Richman 1970:49) of a study of frequently used lexical items, and a low degree of recognizability characterizes infrequently-used lexicon as well ("Such a phenomenon is due to the fact that French has undergone much more extensive vowel evolution and syllabic attrition than its sisters" – Richman 1970:54).

Degrees of diversity in one area are likely indicators that differences exist in other areas as well. That it is not possible to speak of complete uniformity of gender assignment between French and Spanish cognate nouns has been intuited for centuries; the earliest reference I have found on the topic is Chantreau (1781:66), who writes (in the orthography of the era): *"En muchas voces de esta especie, no conviene en el género el castellano con el francés; esto es, que unas son del genero masculino en castellano, y del femenino en francés; ó al contrario..."* Chantreau's work – sophisticated even by modern standards – was apparently not followed up, since thorough searches of bibliographies and one major university library's collection have unearthed no scholarly work comparing French and Spanish noun gender and few if any treatises or manuals of a nonscholarly or pedagogical orientation.[1] It thus appears that the topic of French/Spanish cognate nouns' gender differences has not yet been dealt with, at least not by scholars. Hence my own decision to investigate the matter. My goal was to determine to what extent a knowledge of the noun-gender system of a particular cognate language (French) would aid in learning the noun-gender system of another (Spanish). What percentage of French nouns had Spanish cognates with identical genders? Which, precisely, were the French and Spanish nouns that though cognate did not share gender? And, were there any significant patterns to be found among gender-divergent cognate nouns?

The source of the corpus I will analyze is García-Pelayo y Gross and Testas 1967, better known as the *Larousse* French-Spanish/Spanish-French dictionary and henceforth referred to as *Larousse 1967*. The section from which I extracted all cognate nouns of differing gender was the first or French-Spanish section, which runs to 783 pages and contains — and the following is a very rough estimate, based on the spot-checked assumption that the average page of this dictionary includes 60 main entries — about 46,500 items. (This figure will not form the basis of any calculations because of its highly approximate nature.)

I examined the first two alphabetical sections of Larousse 1967 — "A" and "B" (pp. 1–115) — for cognate nouns, which I classified as either "same gender" or "different gender". Automatically eliminated from consideration were proper names and gender ambivalent ("common gender") nouns which of course take either gender according to the sex of the person referred to. I then continued examining Larousse 1967's remaining alphabetical sections ("C" through "Z," pp. 116–783) only for those cognate nouns that were of different gender. Next I added up all "same gender" nouns and all "different gender" nouns from pp. 1–115 of Larousse 1967, then multiplied the totals by 7 to achieve an approximate idea as to the entire number of same-gender and different-gender noun cognates between the two languages. (The figure 7 is the multiplicand because 115 pp. constitutes 14.69% of the total 783 pp. and is thus within less than a half a percentage point — .40 to be exact — of the fraction 1/7 (100 divided by 7 = 14.29%). Pp. 1–115 of Larousse yielded 1,975 same-gender cognates and 163 different-gender cognates. When these figures are multiplied by 7, we end up with 13,825 same-gender and 1,141 different-gender cognate nouns as our approximate totals for the entire 783 pp. French-Spanish dictionary. While these totals are approximations only, I am satisfied that they represent close and not distant approximations to reality. Because I tallied and then typed up all different-gender cognates, an exact

---

[1] It is possible that the Spanish Biblioteca Nacional may contain the sort of manuals or treatises of a more or less pedagogical nature that are no longer available in bookstores and that would not normally form part of a research library's collection. The French *Bibliothèque Nationale* should also be visited for the works of a similar sort it is sure to contain.

count of that category was possible. It totaled 1,137 items, just 4 fewer than the close estimate I achieved by multiplying 163 by 7.

In order to determine, if only roughly, the degree to which French and Spanish nouns are cognate, I added 13,825 (my close estimate of same gender cognates) and 1,141 (my ibid. of different gender cognates), which gave 14,966. I then compared this total with the figure 4,875, which is my rough estimate of the total number of noncognate nouns in Larousse 1967. (The 4,875 figure was arrived at by identifying then tabulating from pp. 1–20 of the dictionary all noun entries totally void of any cognate relationship. There were 125 of them. The number 125 was then multiplied by 39 (20 x 39 = 780, i.e., as near as possible to 783, the lexicon's total number of pages.) French-Spanish cognate nouns' 14,966 total equals 75.43% of the total 19,841 nouns I have estimated are included in the lexicon. Approximately three out of every four French nouns, then, have Spanish cognates and of course vice versa, and of the cognates, approximately 92.38% are same gendered vs. 7.62% which are different gendered. Thus, given the extent to which Spanish and French are cognate (ca. 75%), examining gender relationships between the two languages' cognates is a useful field of study. And while an overwhelming majority (just over 92%) of French-Spanish cognates are same gendered, enough (nearly 8%) are different gendered for these to merit further study. (See Table 1 for a numerical encapsulation of the statistics just discussed). When asked, then, whether French nouns are a help in learning Spanish nouns and vice versa, the answer is Yes, but. Let us now examine the "but."

My examination of different-gendered French-Spanish cognates took the following tack: I divided them into five groups according to the nature of the items which constituted the particular lexical entry. The groups are: SEC (sole equivalent cognate), SECNOC (sole equivalent cognate plus noncognate(s)), MEC (multiple equivalent cognate), and MECNOC (multiple equivalent cognate plus noncognate(s)). A smattering of nonconforming items are labeled "OTHER." Let me now define and discuss these groups.

SEC (sole equivalent cognate): A one-to-one relationship between two cognate items. Example: (French) *amulette f.* / (Spanish) *amuleto m.* (Since the dictionary section examined was French-Spanish in direction, French items always precede Spanish.) SEC pairs are the simplest to identify, and also constitute a plurality among the five groups at 41.60% with 473/1,137 total. It should be noted that SEC includes sets containing more than one cognate equivalent provided that within the particular language, all equivalents are of the same gender, e.g., *défilé f.* / *desfiladero m., desfile m.* There are only 35 such sets, about half of whose members differ only in spelling, e.g., *fléole f., phléole f.* / *fleo m.*

SECNOC (sole equivalent cognate plus noncognate(s)): A lexical entry containing a one-to-one cognate pair plus one or more noncognate items that

TABLE 1. COUNTS AND PERCENTAGES
FROM LAROUSSE 1967 (Pages 1–783 "French-Spanish" section)

Cognates:

Same gender cognates, pp. 1–115 ("A" and "B"): 1975 (exact count)

Different gender cognates, same source: 163 (exact count)

2,138 TOTAL

Extrapolations of the above counts (x 7 to approximate their totals for the lexicon as a whole):

$1,975 \times 7 = 13,825$ (approximate total, same gender cognates)

$163 \times 7 = 1,141$ (approximate total, different gender cognates)

14,966 TOTAL

Percentages:

(same gender cognates) $13,825 = 92.38\%$ of 14,966 (total cognates in lexicon)

(different gender cognates) $1,141 = 7.62\%$ of 14,966 (total ...)

Noncognates (pp. 1–20, Larousse 1967):

Total noncognates: 125

125×39 (wherein 39 = multiplicand required to extrapolate 20

= pp. onto the lexicon's 783 pp. total)

4,875 (= approximate number of noncognates in the lexicon)

Combined totals:

14,996 (approximate total, all cognates in the lexicon)

4,875 (approximate total, all noncognates in the lexicon)

19,841 (approximate number of nouns in lexicon)

are synonymous, and not included in my list. Example: *accueil m. / acogida f., recibimiento* m. The 273 SECNOC sets on my list constitute 24.01% of the total 1,137.

MEC (multiple equivalent cognate): This category's entries do not constitute a simple one-to-one cognate pair; for a set to be classed as MEC, at least one gender must be represented on both sides of the diagonal line dividing the languages. Example: *bronzage m. / bronceadura f. (bronceado m.)*. Two of these three cognates are masculine; thus, considerations of gender are not a factor when one passes from one language to another (unlike *accueil* ⇔ *acogida*, where it is not possible to pick a same gender cognate). Gender considerations are indeed a factor when passing between the two cognates that are not same gendered (*bronzage* ⇔ *bronceadura*), yet it is one of little concern for the language learner, who is always free to "avoid" the different gendered cognate in favor of its same-gendered cousin. MEC sets are thus of little interest to the analyst of cross-language noun gender, especially if the analysis is pedagogically oriented. Statistics: 217 MEC sets constituting 19.09% of the 1,137 grand total.

MECNOC (multiple equivalent cognate plus noncognate(s)): Like MEC, MECNOC's entries are variegated in gender and do not constitute a simple cognate pair, and, like SECNOC, (the other "-NOC" group), contain one or more synonymous noncognate items alongside the cognate pair itself. Example: *compromission f.* (*compromis m.*) / *compromiso m.*, *comprometimiento m.* The "NOC" (noncognate) components of these lexical entries are again not included in my list, as was also the case with SECNOC's, but for those interested I give them here: (French) *arrangement m.*, (Spanish) *arreglo m.*, *acomodo m.* While strict semantic criteria would argue against including *compromiso* and *comprometimiento* as synonyms as Larousse 1967 does, and, therefore, as equally acceptable translations of the French *compromission*, the present paper's central focus on gender and cognate relationships and how these affect and are affected by noun gender have militated against my paying any more heed to nuance than does Larousse 1967 itself, which lists the two entries *compromis* and *compromission* as follows:

compromis . . . m. *Compromiso, convenio* (transaction). . . . // *Término medio.*

compromission f. *Compromiso*, m, *comprometimiento* m. // *Arreglo*, m. (arrangement).

It is true that *comprometimiento* as defined by the *Diccionario de la lengua española* 1984:349 is the "*acción y efecto de comprometer o comprometerse*" while *compromiso* is defined variously by the same work as "*delegación que para proveer ciertos cargos eclesiásticos o civiles* . . .; *convenio entre litigantes* . . .; *escritura o instrumento en que las partes otorgan este convenio; obligación contraída* . . .; *dificultad, embarazo, empeño* . . ." Nevertheless these minor distinctions are of minimal import to a bilingual, nondefining dictionary such as Larousse 1967, and are even more peripheral to a study such as the present one. MECNOC in any event is the smallest of the four main categories: 156 sets = 13.72% of the total 1,137.

The "OTHER" category (18 sets = 1.58% of total) is limited exclusively to "double-gender" items such as the well known *frente* f. ('forehead') and *frente* m. ('front'), both of which are rendered in French by *front* m., or else to "gender-ambiguous" i.e., "undecided" items such as *casete*, which is either masculine or feminine with no change in meaning. (In effect the language has yet to make up its mind as to what the gender of the noun should be.)

TABLE 2. STATISTICS FROM APPENDIX B
'Alphabetical Listing of Gender-Divergent Cognates'.

SEC: 473 sets (41.60%)

SEC + SECNOC: 65.61%

SECNOC: 273 sets (24.01%)

MEC: 217 sets (19.09%)

MEC + MECNOC: 32.81%

MECNOC: 156 sets (13.72%)

GRAND TOTAL: 1,137 sets
(= 100.00%)

OTHER: 18 sets (1.58%)

Subsequent discussion of French-Spanish gender-divergent cognates will be limited to just two of the four major groups — SEC and SECNOC — since only these two are of significant interest to knowers of the one language desirous of learning the other's gender system. For purposes of analysis I have combined SEC and SECNOC into a single category. There are "pure" as well as "applied" linguistic reasons for this decision. Learners who find the present study of value for the information it provides about the gender difference between French *apostrophe* (f.), for example, and Spanish *apóstrofe* (m.) or *apóstrofo* (also m.) will not find it of interest to know that because one can also say *dicterio* rather than *apóstrofe* as a Spanish translation of *apostrophe*, this particular set is SECNOC, not SEC. SEC and SECNOC are thus merged; the resultant category contains 746 sets or 65.61% of the total 1,137.

The combined SEC/SECNOC categories' sets were then analyzed in terms of suffixation patterns. Three subcategories resulted: "d" (different suffix in the French cognate than in the Spanish cognate), "s" (same suffix in both French and Spanish cognates), and "− −" (no suffixational relationship between cognates). The term "suffix" is limited to productive bound morphemes employed in French or Spanish to form lexical items, and the bound morpheme in question must be used as a suffix in at least one if not both of the items in a given set. What is more, the bound morpheme must be used suffixationally in the particular lexical item in question and not just generally throughout the language. Thus a set like *acrotère* m. / *acrótera* f. (or *acrotera* as the *Diccionario de la lengua española* 1984 gives it) has been classified as "− −" because although both *ère* and *era* are productive suffixes in modern French and Spanish respectively and especially in Spanish (cf. French *quadrilatère,* Spanish *tortillera*), the formation of *acrotère/acrótera* predates the neo-Latin age: both are derived from Latin *acroteria* which in turn is a Hellenism (*akrotérion*). Also rejected as participating in a suffixational relationship were sets such as *aéronef* m. / *aeronave* f.; here, clearly, *nef* and *nave* are not bound-morpheme suffixes but suffixless nouns which can and do stand "unbound" as lexical items in their own right (*la nef, la nave*). Note that noun-noun compounds are classed as "d" if the second noun contains a bound suffix; thus *héliogravure* f. / *heliograbado* m. Examples follow of each of the three subcategories: "d" — *annihilation* f. / *aniquilamiento* m.; "s" — *anagramme* f. / *anagrama* m.; " – – " *anchois* m. / *anchoa* f.

Table 3 encapsulates statistical information from Appendix C ("Alphabetical Listing of SEC and SECNOC Sets .. ").

TABLE 3. STATISTICS FROM APPENDIX C
"Alphabetical Listing of SEC and SECNOC Sets
According to Patterns of Suffixation."

"d" (different suffix in French cognate
than in Spanish cognate):   260 = 34.85%

"s" (same suffix in both French and
Spanish cognates):   53 = 7.11%

" – – " (no suffixational relationship):   433 = 58.04%

TOTALS: 746 = 100.00%

Analysis of the combined SEC/SECNOC corpus reveals that few if any significant relational patterns exist. Among "d" nouns I had hoped to find, for example, large numbers of French items ending in *tion* whose Spanish cognates ended in *m(i)ento*, on the order of *annihilation* f. / *aniquilamiento* m.; there are exactly nine. For every French *ment* / Spanish *ción* set (to reverse the equation), there appears to be a French *tion* / Spanish *m(i)ento*. Only two types of relational patterns achieve anything close to salience. The first occurs in subcategory " – – " (no suffixational relationship), and involves 50 sets all of whose constituent items end in *a* in both languages; examples: *acacia* m. / *acacia* f.; *agenda* m. / *agenda* f.; *alisma* m. / *alisma* f.; *alpaga* m. / *alpaca* f. Since most French *a*-final nouns are masculine and the overwhelming number of Spanish *a*-final nouns are feminine, this particular relational pattern should come as no surprise. Indeed, of the 50 such sets in the present corpus, all French items are masculine and all Spanish items are feminine; there are no exceptions. The second relational pattern — French *eur* nouns as feminine vs. Spanish cognate *or* nouns that are masculine — is well known to

Romance philologists and students of Spanish and French in general; de Dardel 1960 discusses the matter at length within the wider context of the gender of all neo-Latin reflexes of Classical Latin *or*, which designated masculine nouns. The *eur* f./*or* m. pattern contains fewer than half the sets that the *a* m./*a* f. pattern does, and is not without its exceptions, yet the 23 words comprising it appear to be more frequently used, so the *eur*/*or* relational pattern would be of greater utility to the language learner. Examples: French *chaleur* f. / Spanish *calor* m., French *faveur* f. / Spanish *favor* m. There are six exceptions to this pattern; four conform to a subpattern in which French *eur* nouns are masculine and their Spanish cognates end in *ora* (example: *capsulateur* / *capsuladora*); the remaining two are *grosseur* f. / *grueso* m., and *labeur* m. / *labor* f., the latter representing a perfect about-switch from what the rule-knower would expect.

In sum, the relationship between one French suffix and another Spanish suffix has little to reveal about cross-language gender relationships save for two small cognate-noun categories: French -*a* m./Spanish -*a* f., and French *eur* f./Spanish *or* m. Also sadly lacking in significance was the outcome of my study of pairing relationships, i.e., whether more French masculines were paired with Spanish feminines or vice versa. (In other words, was the masculine total higher than the feminine total on the French or on the Spanish side of the diagonal line?) Findings: while somewhat more French feminines were paired with Spanish masculines than the reverse among "d" sets, the reverse was faintly true among " – – " sets and "s" sets, but a summation of all three types of sets reveals only six more French feminines paired with Spanish masculines than the opposite. Thus nothing whatsoever can be concluded from such a study, save that in their very modest feminine predominance, single-equivalent cognates deviate a bit from expected norms. (Recall from Teschner and Russell 1984 that more Spanish nouns are masculine than feminine; the same is true of French to a somewhat higher degree.)

I am mildly disappointed by the outcome of my work on gender relationships between French and Spanish cognates. It is true that my study has expanded knowledge in a number of areas. For example, we now know (as we did not before) that approximately 75% of all French nouns have Spanish cognates and vice versa. We also know — and this is again new knowledge — that slightly more than 92% of all French/Spanish cognates are of the same gender. From my examination of the remaining 8% we now know that a plurality of them (473 = 41.60% of the total 1,137) are sole equivalent cognates like *accueil* m. / *acogida* f., that the next-largest single category (sole equivalent cognates plus noncognate(s)) contains 273 sets at 24.01% of the total, and that together these kindred categories equal nearly two-thirds of the gender-divergent cognate lexicon. What we do not know is whether that circumstance makes any difference, theoretical or pedagogical. We know that a close examination of the 746 sets of the combined SEC and SECNOC categories turns up just two relational patterns of rather minor import, and no more than two. What we are forced to conclude about the 746 cognate sets is that their value is intrinsic "only," though perhaps in light of everything my investigations reveal has not been researched about the topic, intrinsic may be quite good enough. At least we now have about as full a list of French/Spanish cognate sets as we are likely to possess until the Larousse 1967 or its competitors are updated and expanded, and someone else attempts a count.

While French remains a "gender-difficult" language, my work has shown that it can be made considerably less difficult if the particular learner already knows Spanish: to already "know" the gender of 92% of the three quarters of the nouns that are cognate, and then to have, as we do now, ready access to a wordlist that sets forth the remaining 8% is a considerable advantage at very least. However, for the knower of Spanish there still remains that 25% of the noun lexicon that is noncognate; and for the student of French who knows neither Spanish, another Romance language, or Latin, no significant part of the French noun's gender system is familiar territory.[2] For the "Romance-less" student, then, the French noun gender system must be presented *ab ovo*. It is precisely to analyses that do not depend on or presume any prior knowledge of the system that I will devote my attention during the remaining part of this paper.

While studies of the relationship between French nouns' shape and French noun gender have been appearing in print since at least the eighteenth century,[3] it was not until the 1960s that scholars first began attempting to extract

---

2 I am deliberately overlooking the unimportant knowledge of French noun gender that speakers of languages such as Dutch, German, Polish, Russian, etc., already possess by virtue of the French words their tongues have borrowed, often with lending-language gender intact, e.g., French-to-German *la cravate* ⇒ *die Krawatte*, *le crédit* ⇒ *der Kredit*. I am likewise making the assumption—valid if the findings of Richman 1970 and others are any indication—that the degree of cognate relationship between Spanish and French is essentially approximated by Portuguese as it relates to French, and is probably exceeded somewhat by Italian and Catalan, not to mention Provençal. Rumanian of course is a different matter altogether.

3 The earliest study I have been able to examine is Chantreau 1781, who discusses French gender in passing in what is otherwise an overall treatise on French grammar for Spanish speakers. Goodluck 1831 is a remarkably thorough but highly atomistic presentation of the rules for determining French noun gender (118 masculine and 95 feminine rules all told.). Akerly 1842 is almost as atomistic if somewhat less thoroughgoing. Ryder 1871 contains a surprisingly astute list of rules—just 12, save for those involving mute *-e*, which are prolix. Ayer 1885 is pessimistic in his emphasis on the futility of attempting to relate form to gender. There are bound to exist many antique manuals and treatises which I lack knowledge of or have been unable to locate. (See footnote 1, above) The reader should bear in mind that my searches were limited to material on hand at two American libraries and their annexes—the Research Library of the University of California at Los Angeles, and the Perry–Castañeda Library of the University of Texas at Austin—stellar institutions both, but not the Bibliothèque Nationale of Paris when it comes to French materials.

French noun gender rules from entire corpora—invariably dictionaries—instead of establishing the rules more or less a priori by seeking examples to confirm hunches or by adding a few impressionistically-derived rules to material borrowed from previous commentators. Our first example of what can be called whole-corpus noun-gender analysis is Polovina 1961, regrettably more of a note than a full-fledged article (it runs to just more than two pages). To support her generalization that French nouns ending in /a/, /wa/ and /ɔ/ "sont généralement masculines" (Polovina 1961:33), the author briefly mentions in a footnote (1961:34) that she has systematically gone through all seven volumes of the Littré Dictionnaire de la Langue Française and the 1958 Nouveau Petit Larousse Illustré. Yet no statistics whatsoever are put forth to support her statements on these and the other three generalizations she makes (on nouns ending in / æ̃ /, / ɔ̃s /, and / sjɔ̃ / respectively). Almost negligent in her speculation, Polovina (1961:34) notes that "... une classification fondée sur la finale phonique est, au moins en partie, possible.... Nous n'avons observé de ce point de vue que quelques finales. En les passant toutes en revue, on trouverait certainment quelque autre règle orale." It is unfortunate that Polovina did not follow through on her own suggestion. A second, equally frustrating pioneer attempt at deriving French noun gender rules from an entire corpus (in this instance the 1,120-page 1969 Petit Larousse) was made by Rossi (1967–68), who arrived at 29 feminine and 25 masculine categories ranging from the ample (/a/ masculine: 2,563 in conformity, 10 exceptions) to the minuscule (/zjɔ̃ / masculine: 5 in conformity, zero exceptions). Rossi's raw statistics appear in no logical order, are unaccompanied by percentages, do not distinguish between levels of significance, include half a dozen aggroupations which show no clear preference for gender (thus Rossi lists /izɔ̃ /, with 5 f. and 6 m. examples, as feminine-preferent), fail to work out any relationship between phonology and orthography (of considerable utility in more than one instance, e.g., /i/ = "i(C)" is m. overwhelmingly, while /i/ = "ie" is overwhelmingly f.), and omit several endings or combinations of endings from consideration altogether. Nevertheless, Rossi pointed the way to what could be done by more experienced linguists.

With the completion of Tucker 1967, and the rapid appearance of articles derived from and supplementing it (Rigault 1968; Tucker et al. 1968; Tucker, Rigault and Lambert 1970; and Rigault 1971), and the eventual publication of Tucker, Lambert and Rigault 1977, it looked as if the long-awaited whole-corpus-based analysis of gender patterns among French nouns had finally been produced. Of chief interest to students of French morphology were the two appendixes appearing in Tucker, Lambert and Rigault 1977 (henceforth TLR 1977): "Appendix 1: Gender French Nouns: List of Tables: Consonantic Endings" (TLR 1977:69–104), i.e., nouns whose word-final phoneme is a consonant, and "Appendix 2 . . . Vocalic Endings" (TLR 1977:105–125), which contains nouns whose final phoneme is a vowel. Based on the findings of an inverse dictionary compiled by the eminent French linguist Bernard Quemada "which consists of all nouns listed in the Petit Larousse [1959] congregated by written ending, and separated according to gender" (TLR 1977:19), the consonantic-endings appendix gives 31 tables plus 7 subtables listing certain categories' exceptions to the rules, and the vocalic-endings appendix contains 18 such tables with no subtables of exceptions. Of the 31 consonantic-ending aggroupations, one is marked in the List of Tables (TLR 1977:67) as all masculine, 19 as predominantly masculine, 10 as predominantly feminine and just one as masculine/feminine; of the 18 vocalic-ending aggroupations, one is all masculine, 10 are predominantly masculine, 4 predominantly feminine, 2 masculine/feminine and one feminine.

Even a rapid look through these two tables turns up problems. The tables limit themselves to raw numbers and subtotals and do not include percentages or even sum totals. Perhaps it was these omissions that enabled the authors to describe as "predominantly masculine" or "predominantly feminine" a wide variety of types whose percentages of conformity to rule can range from the high 90s to the low 50s. Thus the user is deprived of the background information that is vital when distinguishing (as one must, for the sake of descriptive power) between degrees of predominance. So while tables III and IV (TLR 1977:70-71) are both listed as "predominantly masculine', table III (last phone /k/, written endings *c(s), ch(s), ck(s),* and *q*) contains 222 m. and 2 f. nouns at 99.11%/.09% respectively, while table IV (last phone /k/, written endings *que, ques*) includes 333 m. and 276 f. nouns at 54.68%/45.32% respectively. Clearly, a more discriminating description was called for if this material were to be put to any sort of analytic use.

Nor were Tucker et al.'s problems as a descriptive instrument limited to its wholesale classification as "predominantly" of categories numerically disparate. In several instances it was possible for me to rearrange TLR categories internally, thereby producing classifications that were more efficient and economical in their descriptive power. Examples of this are the consonantic Tables VI (TLR 1977:73), XIV (81-82), XVIII (85), XXVIII (98-99), and vocalic Tables XVII (117), XVI (118-119) and XVIII (120-125). This last table, which TLR flatly label "feminine" (not even "predominantly feminine") in the List of Tables for Appendix 2 (TLR 1977:105), is a fine example of the underanalysis that is often let slip by. Table XVIII ("Last phone: $\tilde{ɔ}$. Written endings: *on, omb* etc.") contains 2669 lexical items, 1883 (70.55%) of which are feminine and 786 (29.45%) masculine. At 70.55% f. predominance, this category as constituted would barely qualify as L(ARGELY) (70-89.9% rule conformity). Reanalyzed, however, the category nicely lends itself to two "overwhelming" classifications: overwhelmingly feminine $-s/t/z/ž$ + $j\tilde{ɔ}$ and $z\tilde{ɔ}$ (written ending *cion/(s)sion/tion/gion/aison* etc.) at 99.46% rule conformity — and overwhelmingly masculine (all remaining /$\tilde{ɔ}$/ endings, i.e., orthographic *ond(s), ons, ong, omb, onc, ont,* and all *on* not *cion/sion* etc.) at 95.41% rule conformity.

The refined analysis which was missing from TLR 1977 was sought in the four spin-off articles (Rigault 1968; Tucker et al. 1968; Tucker, Rigault and Lambert 1970; and Rigault 1971) that were mentioned above, but to a large extent such analysis was sought in vain. Rigault's first article (1968:38-39) contains a brief discussion of the need to include penultimate and antepenultimate phones in any analysis of the relationship between nouns' genders and their word-final elements, and he illustrates his point with three tables which exemplify but hardly exhaust the topic. (There is also no attempt to relate orthography with phonology.) Rigault 1971 repeats some of the same information as part of a longer treatment of French gender marking in general – adjectives and determiners as well as nouns. Tucker, Rigault and Lambert 1970 limits its statistical analysis of noun gender to the word-final phone and to illustrative, tantalizing graphs (1970:282-283) that give just a glimpse of what can be done (and which again fail to take orthography into account).[4] Nor can we turn to Tucker 1967 (the dissertation), available only as a photocopy from the sponsoring university's library, for the analysis we cannot find in TLR 1977 or elsewhere. The dissertation lacks gender-listing appendixes entirely, though it does provide one brief table (1967:14) that relates just ten noun endings to noun-gender predominance types.

It was a close examination of this brief table that made me aware of an even more serious problem with TLR 1977: their appendixes did not include an unspecifiable but clearly substantial number of noun-gender categories sharing /r/ as the word-final segment following vowel. While Table XXII lists all 512 instances of "Consonant + *re(s)*," omitted entirely from consideration in TLR 1977 were all French nouns which end in such commonly-occurring terminations as /war/, /ɑ̃ r/, /ɛr/, /ir/, /œr/, /yr/, etc. Since complete statistics for these categories were nowhere to be found in any published source, it was necessary to consult the unpublished, microfilmed Ursprung of TLR 1977's appendixes: the Quemada (1966?) inverse dictionary of French nouns.

What became apparent when I checked the several dozen charts that appear at the beginning of the Quemada microfilm was that Quemada and not

---

[4] The authors themselves provide evidence in Tucker et al. 1968:315 of the importance of relating sounds to spellings; thus: "The difference found between *aie* and *ais* in gender assignment [by the student subjects being tested for ability to properly assign gender to French nouns both bona fide and invented – a topic which admittedly interested Tucker and his colleagues more than did the morphological analysis of French noun gender patterns] due to method of presentation [aural vs. written] may be explained by noting that the ending /ɛ/ of which *aie* and *ais* are allophones [sic] occurs predominantly in masculine nouns (564 M, 61 F). The ending spelled *aie*, however, as we noted, is found exclusively in feminine nouns."

Tucker et al. had committed the original sin of omission (which Tucker, Lambert and Rigault repeated by accepting Quemada's charts uncritically). Though *r*-final nouns potentially groupable into nearly a dozen categories appear on pp. 213–256 of Quemada, only one such category—the already-mentioned "*C* + *re(s)*"—shows up on the charts. It was necessary for me, then, to complete Quemada's (and Tucker et al.'s) work by examining the contents of pp. 213–256 so as to determine which categories the remaining *r*-final nouns lent themselves to.[5] Examination and analysis produced seven in addition to Quemada's and Tucker et al.'s '*C* + *re(s)*': *V* + *r(s)*; *ière*; two separate divisions of *C* + *ère*; *aire*; *ure*; and "all V = r not covered in the six preceding categories" (chiefly -*are*, *C* + *ire*, *oire*, *ore*, *a/e/ie/i/eu/ou* + *rre*; *aure*; *eure*) (see Appendix D below for details). All told, 4,712 nouns were added to the corpus by including what Quemada and Tucker et al. had omitted. As can be seen, French nouns ending in -*r* do not lend themselves to neat categorization. This is largely so because so many of them (2,165 = 41.44% of 5,224, which is the total number of *r*-final nouns in the corpus) end in mute *e*.

Producing gender rules for nouns which end in the letter *e* (mute) is at the very heart of the problem of noun-gender analysis in French. It is well known that in modern French, alone among standard neo-Latin languages, the "mute *e*" (orthographically *e*, phonetically zero) has replaced first declension final-syllable *a(m)* (thus Latin *rosam* ⇒ French *la rose*) and second declension final-syllable *u(m)* (thus Latin *librum* ⇒ French *le livre*). Consequently, the ubiquitous word-final *a/o* or *u* distinctions, so helpful in the mastery of noun gender in Portuguese, Spanish, Italian and Rumanian, are

---

5 It may well be wondered why I did not simply abandon Quemada/Tucker et al. at this point and concentrate my efforts instead on statistics obtainable from Juilland 1965, an inverse dictionary of French which unlike Quemada (1966?) is available in print, not microfilm. I had been acquainted with Juilland 1965 for as long as I had known of TLR 1977. Before I began the present study it appeared I might do well to base my analyses on the Juilland corpus or, preferably (given time constraints), seek out whatever publications had already done so. (Juilland 1965 gives corpus only, not analysis.) My bibliographic research turned up no publication whose analysis of French noun gender is based on Juilland 1965. What is more, I was dissuaded from any plans to compile my own statistics from Juilland 1965 by the comments of Dudrap and Emery (1971:87-88), who, in the course of describing for an audience of computer scientists an on-going and (as of spring 1987) not-yet-published machine analysis of the contents of the 1969 *Nouveau Petit Larousse,* had the following remarks to make about Juilland 1965:
"[it] seemed to be the most suitable list to work on, giving both grammatical category and nominal gender. Unfortunately this seemingly very scholarly work is totally unreliable, both in its inclusion and exclusion of items (no reference to the origin of the lexical material is given) and, more disturbingly, in its often mistaken attribution of genders."
Hence my decision to retain TLR 1977 as supplemented by Quemada.

almost totally absent in French. As the mute *e* is the French reflex of the word-final marker of such vast numbers of Latin nouns, it is no surprise that nearly half of all French nouns (15,145 of 31,943 = 47.41%; see Appendix E below for further details) end in mute *e*. (These and all subsequent figures on French noun gender have been excerpted or for the most part compiled directly by me from TLR 1977 as supplemented by my compilations from Quemada 1966(?).)

Word-final mute *e* is the massive log jam in what would otherwise be the fast-flowing stream of French noun gender analysis. That fact has been recognized and at times nicely discussed by authors such as Goodluck 1831, Ryder 1871, Byrne and Churchill 1956, Catach 1980, and especially Luce 1979. (This last study is of particular utility, as its very title punningly suggests—"Learning French Genders with 'e's'.") My Appendix E's statistics reveal that only 45.26% of mute *e* nouns belong to categories whose members" rule conformity is "overwhelming" (90–100%): thus there are four overwhelmingly masculine categories of mute *e* nouns, 3,043 (93.23%) of whose total 3,264 components are masculine, and eight overwhelmingly feminine categories of mute *e* nouns, 3,439 (95.63%) of whose total 3,596 components are feminine. If one adds to these all mute *e* nouns forming part of the "L(ARGELY)" (70–89.9% rule conformity) categories, one does not quite manage to achieve two-thirds coverage of all mute *e* nouns in the language: 10,002/15,145 = 66.04%. (There are 3,142 L nouns and 6,860 "overwhelming" nouns = 10,002.)

Thus about 45% of French mute *e* nouns are powerfully describable for gender (though not economically, since 12 categories are required to do so), and another 21% are somewhat less powerfully describable. (Percentages of rule conformity range from 88.42% in the case of *ure* nouns, through 73.54% in the case of *che(s)* nouns; there are six feminine-predominant and three masculine-predominant categories.) The remaining 5,143 = 33.96% of French mute *e* nouns are "M(OOT)" *e* nouns, i.e., they belong to categories whose percentage of rule conformity is lower than 70%, and there are eleven such categories all told, ranging from a high 69.15% to a very low 50.50% rule conformity. It is a cliché of French noun gender discussion to postulate a relationship between word-final mute *e* and the feminine gender, yet only a handful of authors (see for example Togeby 1982:18) are aware of how limited this relationship is. Thus my statistics show (see Appendix E) that just 56.23% (8,516/15,145) of French mute *e* nouns are feminine, leaving a healthy 43.77% (6,629/15,145) as masculine. That there is a certain connection between "feminine" and "mute *e*" can be appreciated by examining the categories in Appendix D (below) and how they relate to each other. That the connection can be described simply and sparingly is not the case at all.

By contrast, gender categorization of nonmute *e* nouns constitutes simplicity itself. Overwhelmingly masculine-gendered are: (1) nouns which end in a consonant grapheme or a consonantal digraph—thus *"b c(s) ch(s) ck(s) q d f(s) g(s) l(s) m n p r s(s) x sh t dj"* including nouns which end in /a/ written *"ac ap at(s) as"* designating numerical singular (cf. /a/ written "a," a masculine-predominant moot category—see Appendix D); (2) nouns ending in tonic /é/ preceded by any sound segment except /t/; and (3) nouns ending in all other vocalic phones (/wa/, /ã/, /ɛ̃/, /i/, /o/, /ɔ̃/, /œ/, /æ/, /y/, /u/, or /ɛ/) provided these are not orthographically represented with word-final mute *e*, or are /ɔ̃/ not preceded by /j/ or /z/. Also overwhelmingly masculine-gendered are: (4) nouns belonging to four word-final mute *e* categories: *me(s)*, orthographic *"b c d f h p r t ou + ère," ste* preceded by /a/, /e/ or /i/, and *ge(s)*.

Approximately half of all French nouns are masculines in conformity with the four rules just presented. (If only the 15,853 masculine nouns conforming to the four rules are included, 49.63% — 15,853/31,943 — of all French nouns' genders can be explained thereby. If exceptions plus rule-conforming items are taken as the basis for calculations, 51.45% — 16,436/31,943 — of all French nouns' genders can be explained by the four rules.)

Overwhelmingly feminine-gendered nouns end in mute *e* or tonic /é/ and belong to the following ten categories, defined orthographically except as noted: (1) *ade/ude(s)* (cf. *de(s)*, a slightly feminine-predominant moot category); (2) *elle* (cf. *(l)le(s)*, a very slightly masculine-predominant moot category); (3) *ine* (cf. *ne(s)*, a feminine-predominant moot category); (4) -*ière* (cf. the overwhelmingly-masculine *ère* category depicted above; cf. also the feminine-predominant L(ARGELY) category consisting of all *C* + *ère* where *C* ≠ as specified for the overwhelmingly masculine category); (5) *se* or *ze*; (6) *ie(s)* or *ye* (cf. the overwhelmingly-masculine category in which /i/ is orthographically represented *ic, id, il, is,* etc.); (7) *ue(s)* (cf. /y/ represented *"u ul us uts"* etc., overwhelmingly masculine); (8) *oue(s)* (cf. /u/ spelled variously as an overwhelmingly masculine category); (9) phonemic /té/ *Cté(s) ter'* or /Cé/ orthographically *Cée*; and (10) *ion* (seldom *yon*) preceded by *"c(s)s t g"* and *aison*. As is evident, rules for feminine nouns lend themselves less well to generalization than do their masculine counterparts—a surprising circumstance when we consider that 62.16% of all French nouns are masculine and only 37.87% are feminine. (It would be inaccurate and misleading to term "mute *e*" a valid generalization because of the larger number of its categories outside the "overwhelmingly" feminine classification than within it, and "tonic /é/" is bifurcated between masculine and feminine "overwhelmings" and in any event refers to just one category within the feminine group.)

The above 14 "overwhelming" (90–100% conformity) rules (four masculine and ten feminine) explain the gender assignment of 72.67% (23,214/31,943) of all French nouns if the exceptions to the rules are factored in, and 70.01% (22,363/31,943) if they are not. In effect, then, slightly less than three out of every four French nouns' genders can be explained by 14 rules. (Recall that the gender of slightly more than 95% of all Spanish nouns can be summed up by just four rules.) Slightly more than 25% of the nouns of French are explained for gender by rules of progressively decreasing powerfulness. However, if we factor in the nine categories of nouns whose 70–89.9% conformity to rule has classified them as L(ARGELY), our rules for gender determination now achieve an 82.51% (26,356/31,943) coverage of the total corpus. (If we exclude all L nouns constituting exceptions to their categories' particular rules, the percentage of nouns covered drops to 78.14% — 24,961/31,943. L noun categories' percentages of rule conformity range from a high of 88.42% to a low of 73.54% with a mean of around 81.50%.) In descending order of conformity to rule, the three masculine-predominant L categories (see Appendix D for additional statistics) are: (1) C + re(s) (81.44% m. predominant); (2) -aire (81.16%); (3) fe(s)/phe(s) (77.10%). In descending order of rule conformity, the six feminine-predominant L categories are: (1) ure (88.42%); (2) V + ille(s) (85%); (3) ce/se/xe (84.59%); (4) oie(s)/oye (76.19%); (5) all C + ère where C ≠ "b c d f h p r t ou" (74.07%); and (6) che(s) (73.54%). Whereas there were 16,436 nouns in masculine-predominant vs. only 6,778 in feminine-predominant categories of the "overwhelming" type, the ratio is largely reversed among L(ARGELY) nouns: 1,004 masculine vs. 2,138 feminine.

An examination for descending order of rule conformity of the 12 categories which constitute our M(OOT) classification (below 70% conformity to rule) reveals a useful gap between the highest-conforming (three categories) and the lowest-conforming (the remaining nine). Here is the top end of the rank order: (1) t{t/h}e(s) (69.15% feminine-predominant); (2) ve(e(s)) (68.53% feminine-predominant); (3) a (68.69% masculine-predominant); (4) gne(s) (60.87% feminine-predominant). (The remaining eight categories' percentages of conformity range from 59.63% to 50.50%.) There thus exists a 7.82 percent gap between a nouns and gne(s) nouns, a fact which when coupled with the size of the t(t)e(s)/t(h)e(s) nouns category — 1,569 constituents, 1,085 of which are feminine — has persuaded me of the usefulness of including the three most rule-conforming M categories among the total to be considered in drawing up a final, rule-ordered list of French noun-gender rules. (See Table 4 below.) Before doing so, however, a brief discussion of the remaining nine M categories will serve to tie up any possible loose ends.

The sole feature held in common by the remaining nine M(OOT) categories is that their constituent elements all end in mute e. Five categories are (slightly) masculine-predominant and four slightly feminine-predominant. A gender-based rank ordering results in the following hierarchy: SLIGHTLY MASCULINE-PREDOMINANT: (1) be(s) (59.63%); (2) all V + re(s) not covered in the previous /r/final categories (see Appendix D for details); predominant orthographic endings are: are, C + ire, oire, ore, rre, *aure, eure)* (58.86%); (3) *gue(s)* (57.53%); (4) *que(s)* (54.70%); and (5) *(l)le(s)* (50.50%). SLIGHTLY FEMININE-PREDOMINANT: (1) *gne(s)* (60.87%); (2) *re(s)* (58.47%); (3) *ne(s)* ≠ *ine* (54.56%); (4) *de(s)* ≠ *ade, ude(s)* (52.66%). Statistics show that while there are more feminine M nouns than masculine (these statistics include all 12 M categories), the difference does not amount to much: 3,015/5,587 f. (53.96%) vs. 2,572/5,587 m. (46.04%).

What now follows is the final, rule-ordered list of form-based French noun-gender rules as extracted and conceptualized from Appendix D. It should be born in mind that the present list aims at a level of generalization somewhere between the theoretical and the pedagogical. Thus while certain details available in Appendix D will be omitted, the end result will not quite be pitched at the audience one might expect to find using, say, an intermediate French-as-a-foreign-language textbook.

Concluding Remarks and Generalizations

While Spanish noun gender has now been reduced to a few brief rule statements that are as powerful and economical as one can probably hope for, French noun gender though examined to my current satisfaction has clearly shown itself to be less amenable to simple analysis. It is hoped that my work has shown both the simplicity of the Spanish system and the complexity of its French equivalent, along, of course, with the degree to which knowledge of Spanish can prove useful in learning the French noun gender system and vice versa.

In the most general of terms – and here we are dealing with the "rules about rules" so beloved by transformationalists – Spanish noun gender can be viewed as "feminine marked" while French noun gender is viewable (though less happily) as "masculine marked'. Once the Spanish rules for assignment of nouns to the feminine gender are specified, the remaining nouns can safely be labeled as indeterminate/moot and then masculine; with feminine and moot out of the way, "all others" are masculine. In French, the opposite occurs: the more economical and powerful – in effect the simpler – categorization of nouns as masculine (4 categories) requires that we perform masculine labeling first and feminine labeling subsequently, with substantial "largely" and "moot" categories as residues. As was noted, feminine nouns enjoy a slight edge over masculine nouns in these categories, which is yet another reason for declaring masculine to be the marked gender in French when discussion of markedness is based on an analysis of form.

TABLE 4
Rule-ordered List Of Form-based French Noun-gender Rules
From Appendix D

(I) OVERWHELMINGLY MASCULINE (90-100% conformity to rule):

(1) Nouns ending in a consonant grapheme or a consonantal digraph:

b c(s) ch(s) ck(s) q d f(s) g(s) l(s) m n p r s(s) x sh t(s) dj

(2) Nouns ending in tonic /é/ preceded by any segment except /t/.

(3) Nouns ending in all other vocalic phones — /wa ã ẽ i o õ œ œ̃ y u ɛ/ — provided these are not orthographically represented by word-final mute e, or are not /õ/ preceded by /j/ or /ɛz/.

(4) Nouns ending in orthographic *me(s)*; in "*b c d f h p r t ou*" + *ère*; in *ste* (preceded by /a e i/); or in *ge(s)*.

(II) OVERWHELMINGLY FEMININE (90-100% CONFORMITY TO RULE):

GENERAL COMMMENT: all such nouns end in mute *e* (23.74% of all mute *e*'s belong to this category, and 53.07% of this category's constituents are mute *e*'s), or tonic /é/ preceded by *t*, or /[j/z] /. Details are:

NOUNS ENDING IN:

(1) *ade/ude(s)*

(2) *elle*

(3) *ine*

(4) *ière*

(5) *se* or *ze*

(6) *ie(s)* or *ye*

(7) *ue(s)*

(8) *oue(s)*

(9) /té/ (orthographically '*té(s)   tée(s)   ter*') or /Cé/ (orthographically *Cée*).

(10) *ion* (seldom *yon*) preceded by '*c (s) t g*' or '*aison*'.

(III) LARGELY MASCULINE (70–89.9% conformity to rule—includes one category whose percentage of conformity is slightly below 70%).

Nouns ending in:

(1) C + *re(s)* (81.44% m.-predominant).

(2) *aire* (81.16%).

(3) *fe(s)* or *phe(s)* (77.10%).

(4) *a* (68.69%).

(IV) LARGELY FEMININE (70.89.9% conformity to rule—includes two categories whose percentage of conformity is slightly below 70%).

Nouns ending in:

(1) *ure* (88.42% f.-predominant).

(2) V + *ille(s)* (85%).

(3) *ce* or *se* or *xe* (84.59%).

(4) *oie*(s) or *oye* (76.19%).

(5) all C + *ère* where C is not orthographic "*b c d f h p r t ou*" (74.07%).

(6) *che(s)* (73.54%).

(7) *t{t/h}e(s)* (mostly *tte*) (69.15%).

(8) *ve(e(s))* (mostly *ve*) (68.53%).

(V) MOOT (i.e., INDETERMINATE AS TO GENDER):

This category consists exclusively of all remaining word-final mute *e* nouns, i.e., all mute *e* nouns not categorized in (I) through (IV) above. In effect, these nouns must be memorized for gender. The nine categories are:

(A) SLIGHTLY MASCULINE-PREDOMINANT:

(1) *be(s)*; (2) V + *re(s)* such as: *are, Cire, oire, ore, rre, aure, eure*; (3) *gue(s)*; (4) *que(s)*; (5) *(l)le(s)* ≠ *elle*.

(B) SLIGHTLY FEMININE-PREDOMINANT:

(1) *gne(s)*; (2) *pe(s)*; (3) *ne(s)* ≠ *ine*; (4) *de(s)* ≠ *ade* or *ude(s)*.

REFERENCES

Akerly, J. 1842. *An essay on the genders of French nouns.* New York: J.F. Trow.

Ayer, C. 1885. *Grammaire comparée de la langue française.* 4th ed. Paris: H. Georg.

Bergen, John J. 1978. "A simplified approach for teaching the gender of Spanish nouns." *Hispania* 61:868–76.

Bull, William E. 1965. *Spanish for teachers.* New York: Ronald.

Byrne, L.S.R. and E.L. Churchill. 1956. *A comprehensive French grammar with classified vocabularies.* 2nd ed. Oxford: Basil Blackwell.

Catach, Nina. 1980. *L'Orthographe française: Traité théorique et pratique avec des travaux d'application et leurs corrigés.* Paris: Nathan.

Chantreau, Pedro Nicolás. 1781. *Arte de hablar bien francés* . . . Madrid: A. de Sancha. 2 vols. in one.

Chevalier, Jean Claude et al. 1964. *Grammaire Larousse du français contemporain.* Paris: Larousse.

de Dardel, Robert. 1960. "Le genre des substantifs abstraits en -or dans les langues romanes et en roman commun." *Cahiers Ferdinand de Saussure* 17:29–45.

Diccionario de la lengua española. V.s. Real Academia Española.

Doman, Mary Gay. 1982. "More on rules for rules: Gender in Spanish and the monitor user." *Foreign Language Annals* 15:9–19.

Dudrap, C. and G. Emery. 1971. "Sorting the French vocabulary according to word endings." *The Computer in literary and linguistic research: Papers from a Cambridge symposium (1970)*, ed. by R.A. Wisbey, 87–92. London: Cambridge University Press.

Faitelson-Weiser, Silvia. 1985. "Un nuevo diccionario inverso de la lengua española: El DILE." *Hispania* 68:341–2.

García-Pelayo y Gross, Ramón and Jean Testas, eds. 1967. *Dictionnaire français-espagnol - espagnol/français Larousse.* Paris: Librarie Larousse. 2 vols. in one.

Goodluck, W.R., Jr. 1831. *The French genders, taught in six fables; being a plain and easy art of memory, by which the genders of 15,584 French nouns may be learned in a few hours.* 20th ed. London: J. Chappel, Royal Exchange.

Grevisse, Maurice. 1980. *Le bon usage: Grammaire française, avec des remarques* .... 11th ed. Gembloux: J. Duculot.

Juilland, Alphonse. 1965. *Dictionnaire inverse de la langage français.* The Hague: Mouton.

Keys, A.C. 1957. "French masculine nouns in *e*: The historical approach to a problem of gender." (Auckland University College Bulletin 52, Modern Language Series 2.) Auckland, New Zealand: Auckland University.

Larousse 1967. V.s. García-Pelayo y Gross and Testas 1967.

Luce, Stanford L. 1979. "Learning French genders with 'e's.' *French Review* 52:567–74.

Polovina, Pera. 1961. "Quelques remarques sur le genre grammatical en français." *Bulletin des Jeunes Romanistes* 3:32–34.

Posner, Rebecca. 1966. *The Romance languages: A linguistic introduction.* Garden City NY: Doubleday/Anchor Books.

Quemada, Bernard. 1966 (?). [*Inverse French dictionary* (microfilm's frontispiece gives no title so this one has been assigned).] Montréal: McLennan Library, McGill University. (Available on microfilm only.)

Real Academia Española. 1984. *Diccionario de la lengua española.* 20th ed. Madrid: Editorial Espasa-Calpe. (18th ed. = 1956.)

Richman, Stephen H. 1970. "Identical spelling and recognizability among Romance cognates." *Studia Linguistica: Revue de Linguistique Générale et Comparée* 24:43–55.

Rigault, André. 1968. "Les marques du genre." *Le Français dans le Monde* 57:37–42.

———. 1971. "Les marques du genre." *La grammaire du français parlé*, ed. by André Rigault, 80–91. Paris: Hachette, 1971.

Rossi, P. Carlo. 1967–68. "French gender by sound." *French Review* 41:340–3.

Ryder, Alb. H. 1871. *The infallible rules to the French genders taught very rapidly and on an entirely new plan.* 6th ed. Paris: C. Leroy.

Stahl, Fred A. and Gary E.A. Scavnicky. 1973. *A reverse dictionary of the Spanish language.* Urbana: University of Illinois Press.

Teschner, Richard V. and William M. Russell. 1984. "The gender patterns of Spanish nouns: An inverse dictionary-based analysis." *Hispanic Linguistics* 1:115–32.

Togeby, Knut. 1982. *Grammaire française*. Vol. 1: Le nom. Copenhagen: Akademisk Forlag.

Tucker, G. Richard. 1967. "French speakers' skills with grammatical gender: An example of rule-governed behavior." Ph.D. Diss., McGill University.

——, Wallace E. Lambert and André Rigault. 1977. *The French speaker's skill with grammatical gender: An example of rule-governed behavior*. The Hague and Paris: Mouton.

——, Wallace E. Lambert, André Rigault and Norman Segalowitz. 1968. "Psychological investigation of French speakers' skill with grammatical gender." *Journal of Verbal Learning and Verbal Behavior* 7:312–6.

——, André Rigualt and Wallace E. Lambert. 1970. "Le genre grammatical des substantifs en français: Analyse statistique et étude psycholinguistique." *Actes du Xe-Congrès International des Linguistes* (Bucharest), vol. 3, pp. 279–90.

Valdman, Albert. 1961. *Applied linguistics: French – A guide for teachers*. Boston: D.C. Heath.

——, 1976. *Introduction to French phonology and morphology*. Rowley MA: Newbury House.

Appendix A:

Statistics from Teschner and Russell 1984

Feminine, 90–100% ('overwhelming') predominance:

	f.	m.	category total
a	15,400 *(96.30%)	591 (3.70%)	15,991
d	1,042 (97.57%)	26 (2.43%)	1,068
	16,442 (96.38%)	617 (3.62%)	17,059

* The figures for f. *a* nouns are closely approximate. All other sums constitute exact counts.

Indeterminate as to Gender = 70–50% conformity to type:

	f.	m.	category total
n	2,273 (51.61%)	2,131 (48.39%)	4,404
z	249 (61.63%)	155 (38.37%)	404
s	483 (42.68%)	649 (57.32%)	1,132
	3,005 (50.59%)	2,935 (49.41%)	5,940

Masculine, 90–100% ('overwhelming') predominance:

1,000 or more nouns per word-final letters:

	m.	f.	category total
l	1,140 (97.85%)	25 (2.15%)	1,165
o	12,536 (99.87%)	16 (0.13%)	12,552
r	1,427 (98.55%)	21 (1.45%)	1,448
e**	2,686 (89.35%)	320 (10.65%)	3,006

** For all practical purposes, *e* can be included in among the "overwhelming" categories (see discussion, p. 80).

30-350 nouns per word-final letters:

	f.	m.	category total
i	309 (93.13%)	23 (6.93%)	332
m	30 (100.00%)	0 (0.00%)	30
t	39 (92.86%)	3 (7.14%)	42
u	97 (95.10%)	5 (4.09%)	102
x	30 (90.91%)	3 (9.90%)	33
y	89 (93.68%)	6 (6.32%)	95

Fewer than 30 nouns per word-final letters:

b, c, ch, f, g, j, k, ll, p (totals and percents. for all 9):

76 (97.44%)	2 (2.56%)	78
18,459 (97.75%)	424 (2.25%)	18,883

APPENDIX B: Alphabetical Listing of Gender-Divergent Cognates. (60 pp. in length.)

APPENDIX C: Alphabetical Listing of SEC and SECNOC Sets According to Patterns of Suffixation. (28 pp. in length.)

The length of these two appendixes has prevented their inclusion in the present volume. Readers desirous of obtaining copies of either appendix or both are invited to write: Richard V. Teschner, Dept. of Languages and Linguistics, UTEP, El Paso TX 79968 USA.

APPENDIX D
Alphabetical Listing Of All French Noun Gender Phonological Categories

MASCULINE 90-100%					FEMININE 90-100%					L(ARGELY) (70-89.9%) or M(OOT) (below 70%)					
phone	grapheme	masc.	fem.	total for category	phone	grapheme	fem.	masc.	total for category	phone	grapheme	fem.	masc.	total for category	predominant gender
b	b	95.00 (19)	5.00 (1)	20						M b	be(s)	40.37 (44)	59.63 (65)	109	m.
k	c(s)	99.10 (222)	.90 (2)	224						M k	que(s)	45.30 (276)	54.70 (333)	609	m.
	ch(s)														
	ck(s)														
q	q														
d	d	97.80 (45)	2.20 (1)	46 (EXCEPT FOR:)	*d	ade / ude(s)	90.64 (213)	9.36 (22)	235	M d	de(s)*	52.66 (228)	47.34 (205)	433	f.
f	f(s)	98.20 (167)	1.80 (3)	170						L f	fe(s), phe(s)	22.90 (30)	77.10 (101)	131	m.
g	g(s)	98.90 (88)	1.10 (1)	89						M g	gue(s)	42.47 (62)	57.53 (84)	146	m.
j	V + il	100.00 (72)	-----	72						L j	V + ille(s)	85.00 (238)	15.00 (42)	280	f.
l	l(s)	99.90 (450)	0.11 (5)	455	l	elle	92.69 (203)	7.31 (16)	219	M l	(l)le(s) ≠ -elle	49.50 (449)	50.50 (458)	907	m.
m	m	99.26 (268)	.74 (2)	270											
m	me(s)	90.14 (1024)	9.86 (112)	1136											
n	n	95.16 (59)	4.84 (3)	62 EXCEPT FOR:	in / ine	96.65 (433)	3.35 (15)	448 EXCEPT FOR:	M n	ne(s) ≠ -ine	54.56 (341)	45.44 (284)	625	f.
ñ										M ñ	gne(s)	60.87 (42)	39.13 (27)	69	f.

112 Current Trends and Issues in Hispanic Linguistics

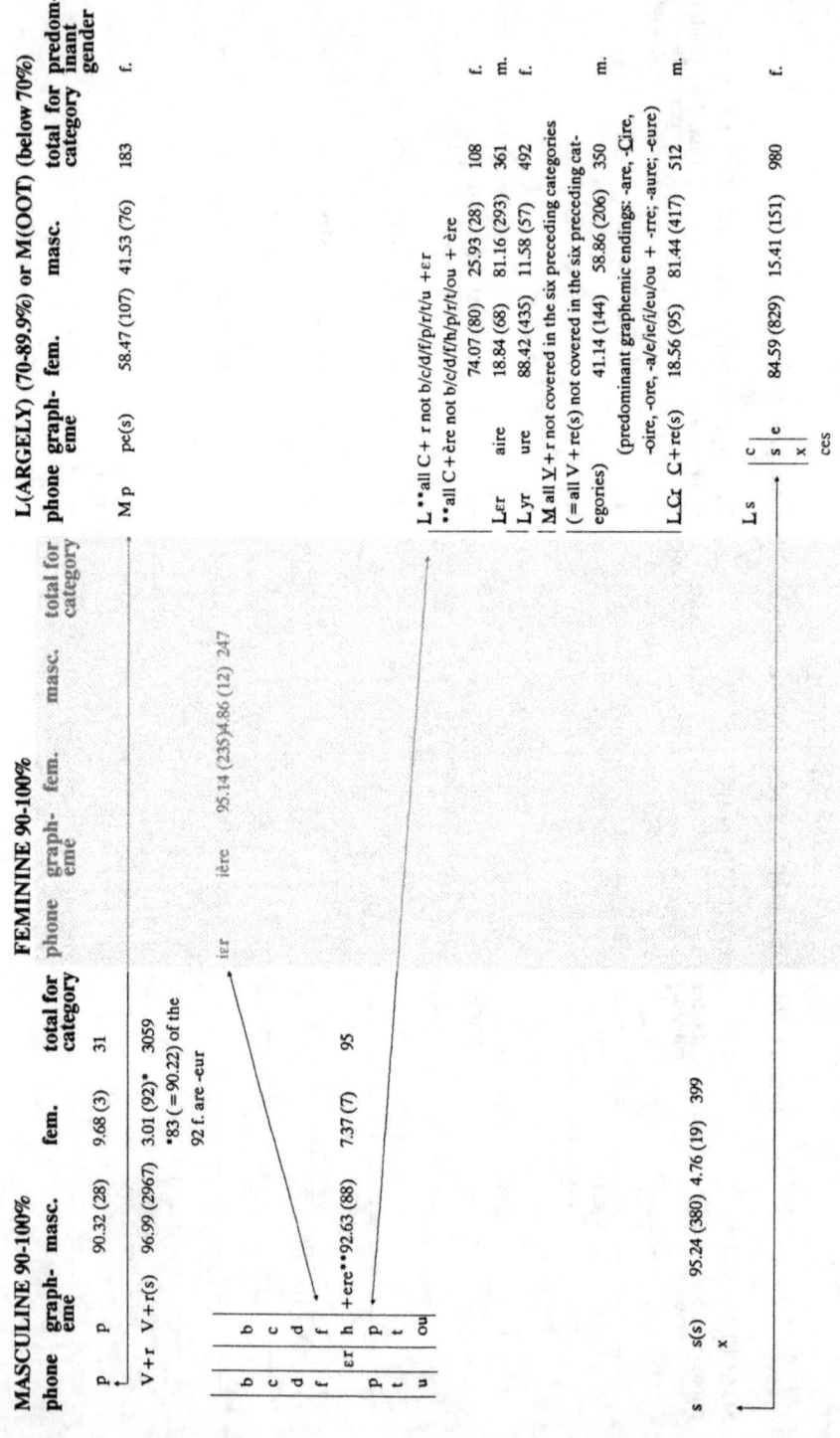

MASCULINE 90-100%

phone	grapheme	masc.	fem.	total for category
p	p	90.32 (28)	9.68 (3)	31
V+r	V+r(s)	96.99 (2967)	3.01 (92)*	3059
			*83 (=90.22) of the 92 f. are -eur	
ɛr	+ere**	92.63 (88)	7.37 (7)	95
s	s(s)	95.24 (380)	4.76 (19)	399
	x			

FEMININE 90-100%

phone	grapheme	fem.	masc.	total for category
iɛr	ière	95.14 (235)	4.86 (12)	247

L(ARGELY) (70-89.9%) or M(OOT) (below 70%)

phone	grapheme	fem.	masc.	total for category	predominant gender
M p	pe(s)	58.47 (107)	41.53 (76)	183	f.
L** all C+r not b/c/d/f/p/r/t/u +ɛr					
**all C+ère not b/c/d/f/h/p/r/t/ou + ère					
		74.07 (80)	25.93 (28)	108	f.
L ɛr	aire	18.84 (68)	81.16 (293)	361	m.
L yr	ure	88.42 (435)	11.58 (57)	492	f.
M all V+r not covered in the six preceding categories (=all V+re(s) not covered in the six preceding categories)		41.14 (144)	58.86 (206)	350	m.
(predominant graphemic endings: -are, -Cire, -oire, -ore, -a/e/ie/i/eu/ou + -rre; -aure, -eure)					
L Cr C+re(s)		18.56 (95)	81.44 (417)	512	m.
L s c / s e / x	ces	84.59 (829)	15.41 (151)	980	f.

Teschner: Noun Gender Categories in Spanish and French 113

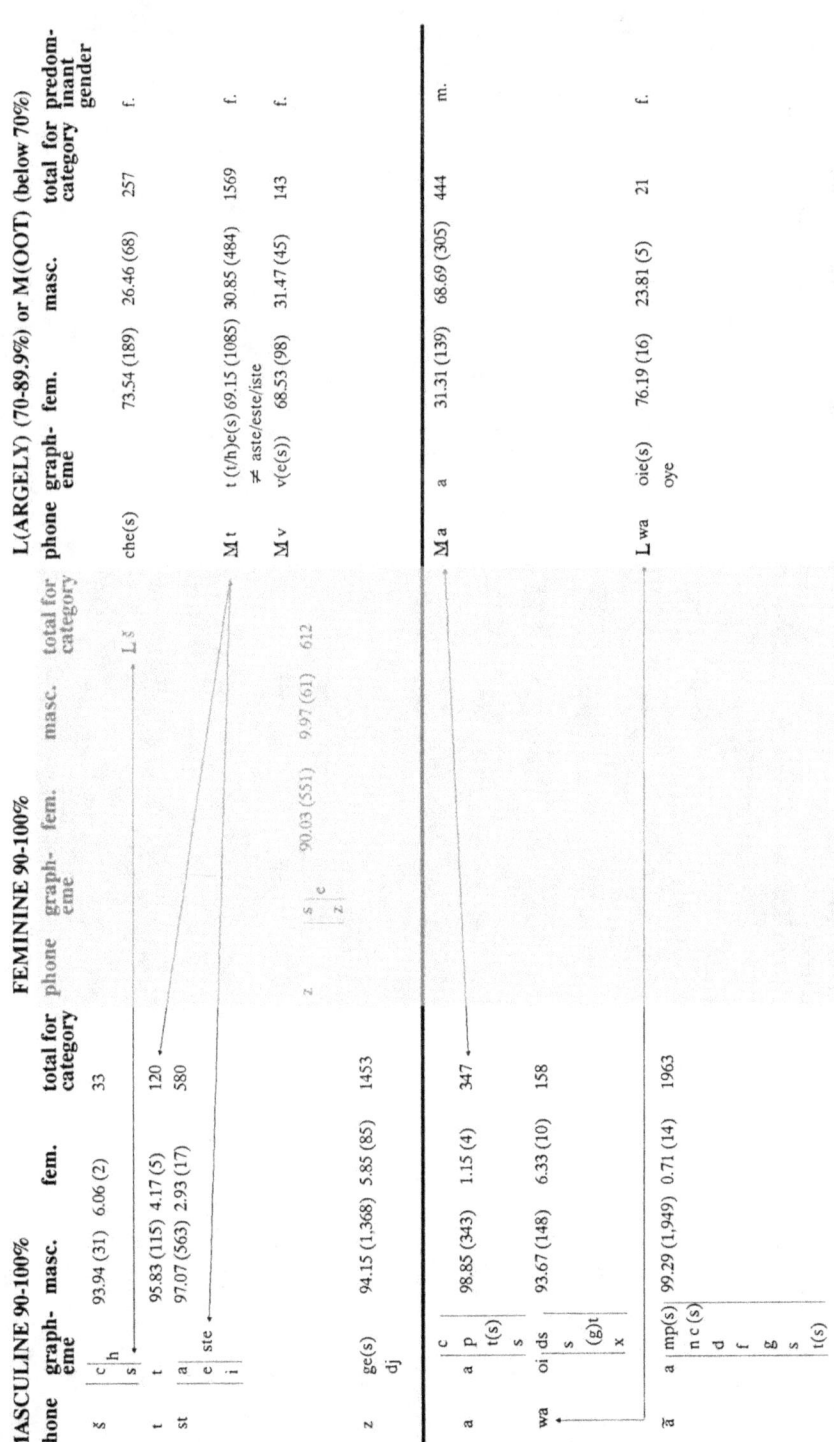

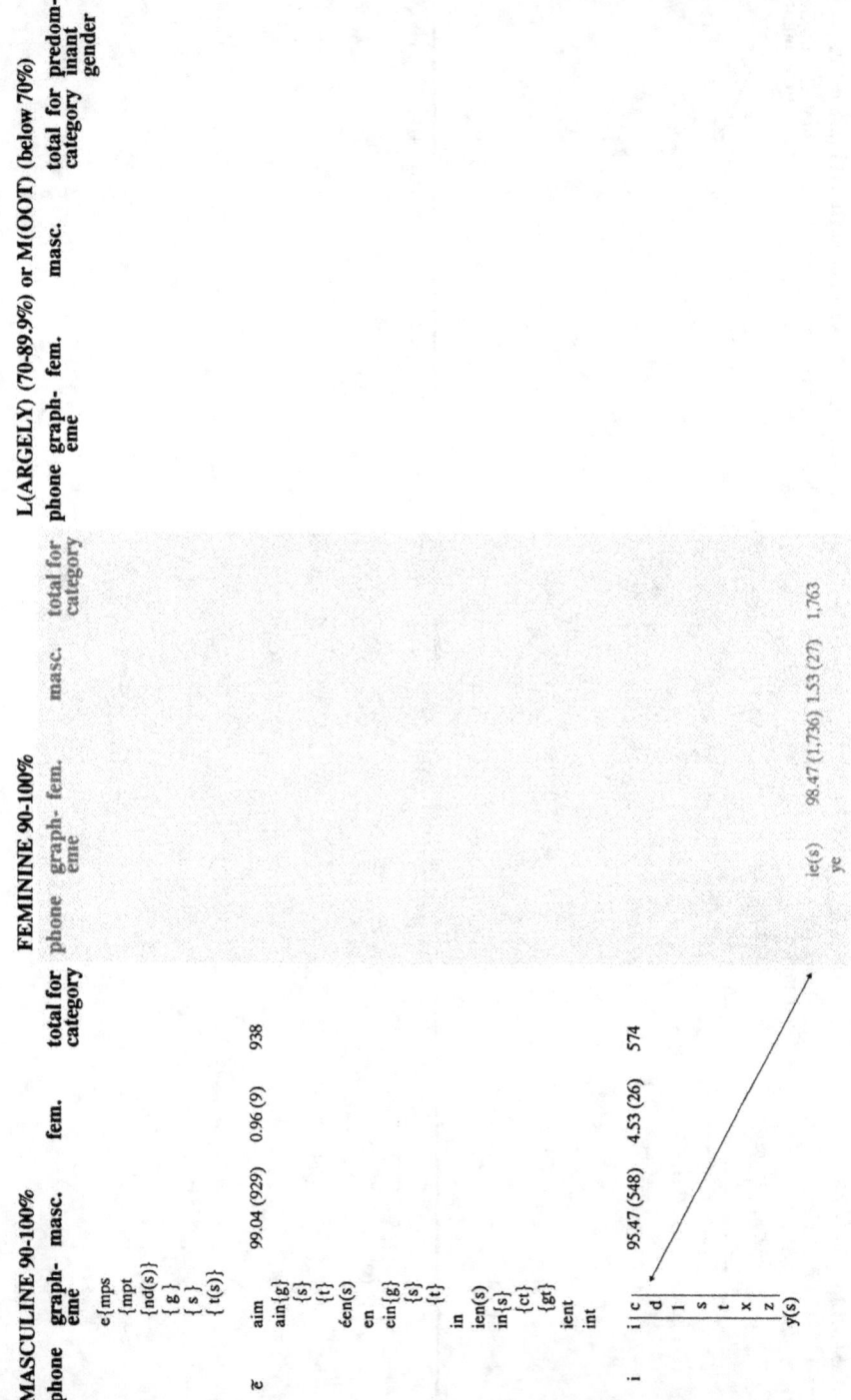

Teschner: Noun Gender Categories in Spanish and French 115

MASCULINE 90-100%					FEMININE 90-100%					L(ARGELY) (70-89.9%) or M(OOT) (below 70%)				
phone	graph-eme	masc.	fem.	total for category	phone	graph-eme	fem.	masc.	total for category	phone	graph-eme	fem.	masc.	total for category / predominant gender
o	o{c} {p} {s} {ts} {t}	97.23 (841)	2.77 (24)	865										
	au{d} {t} {lt} {x} {lx}													
au / eau (x)														
œ	œu{d} {fs}	97.35 (184)	2.65 (5)	189										
	eu{e} {t} {x} eu													
œ̃	u{m} {n(s)} {n (t)}	100.00 (17)	------	17										
y	u{l} {s} {ts} {t} {x}	96.62 (143)	3.38 (5)	148	y	uc(s)	98.11 (52)	1.89 (1)	53					

MASCULINE 90-100%

phone	grapheme	masc.	fem.	total for category
u	o|u u|c i p s t ls x	96.71 (147)	3.29 (5)	152
a	i is it its ix ie* ies y	9,024(564)	976(61)	625
e	t(s) ct(s) y êt ès			

*is all -aie = f. nouns are factored out, the percentage of m. is even higher: 9384 m. vs. 616 f.

FEMININE 90-100%

phone	grapheme	fem.	masc.	total for category
u	oue(s)	84.21 (16)	15.79 (3)*	19

*All three m. exceptions are compounds, hence my decision to include this otherwise f. category in among the overwhelmings. (The overwhelming majority of French compounds are masculine.)

L(ARGELY) (70-89.9%) or M(OOT) (below 70%)

phone	grapheme	fem.	masc.	total for category	predominant gender

Teschner: Noun Gender Categories in Spanish and French

MASCULINE 90-100%

phone	grapheme	masc.	fem.	total for category
e				
(2) i	i + é(s)	9802 (792)	198 (16)	808
j	ée(s)			
	er(s)			

(3) C (≠t) + e

All other written endings, i.e., C (≠t) +

	é	9842 (373)	158 (6)	379
	és	10000 (68)	----	68
	er	10000 (61)	----	61
	ers	10000 (1)	----	1; also:
	quai, nez	10000 (2)	----	2
		9883 (505)	117 (6)	511

(All remaining /ɔ̃/—overwhelmingly -on ≠ -cion/sion/tion etc. supra, with small numbers of -ond(s), -ons, -ong, -omb, -onc, and -ont.)
95.41 (789) 4.59 (38) 827

FEMININE 90-100%

phone	grapheme	fem.	masc.	total for category
		9246 (1239)	754 (101)	1340

(To analyze this complex category's constituents in a way that is both powerful and economical, attention must be paid to written endings alike, leading to the establishment of the following hierarchy:

(1) te — té(s)
tée(s)
ter
Ce — Cée

s / ʃ	cion/(ç)sion/tion
t	tion/tyon
z, ʒ	sion
	gion FOR ALL FIVE GROUPS:
ɛʒ ɔ̃	aison 99.46 (1832) .54 (10) 1842

L(ARGELY) (70-89.9%) or M(OOT) (below 70%)

phone	grapheme	fem.	masc.	total for category	predominant gender

APPENDIX D (STATISTICS/ALPHABETICAL LISTING)
Statistics From 'Alphabetical Listing Of All French Noun Gender Phonological Categories':

MASCULINE 90-100% – 32 categories:
total m.:   15,853 = 96.45%
total f.:   583 =   3.55%
sum total: 16,436 = 100.00%

FEMININE 90-100% – 10 categories:
total m.:   268 =   3.95%
total f.:   6,510 = 96.05%
sum total: 6,778 = 100.00%

L(ARGELY) (70-89.9%) – 9 categories:
m. predominance: m.: 811 = 80.78%   Total L m.'s:
(3 categories)   f.: 193 = 19.22%   1,162 = 36.98%
                1,004 = 100.00%

f. predominance: m.: 351 = 16.42%   Total L f.'s:
(6 categories)   f.: 1,787 = 83.58%   1,980 = 63.02%
                2,138 = 100.00%
                                        3,142 = L sum total

M(OOT) (below 70%): 12 categories

m. predominance: m.: 1,451 = 56.57%   Total M m.'s:
                 f.: 1,114 = 43.43%   2,572 = 46.04%
                    2,565 = 100.00%

f. predominance: m.: 1,121 = 37.10%   Total M f.'s:
                 f.: 1,901 = 62.90%   3,015 = 53.96%
                    3,022 = 100.00%
                                        5,587 = M sum total

COMBINED L + M totals: 21 categories

L + M m.'s: 3,732 = 42.78%
L + M f.'s: 4,995 = 57.22%
            8,729 = 100.00%

Teschner: Noun Gender Categories in Spanish and French 119

GRAND TOTALS (all three columns, i.e., MASC. 90-100, FEM. 90-100, and combined LARGELY and MOOT):

total m.: 15,853
268
3,734
19,855 = 62.16%

total f.: 583
6,510
4,995
12,088 = 37.84%

total m. + f.: 31,943 = 100.00%
(The sum '31,943' thus constitutes the total number of nouns in Tucker et al./Quemada corpus.)

MASC. 90-100 m.'s as % of total corpus (% of nouns in rule-conformity to MASC. 90-100's m. rules): 15,853/31,943 = 49.63%
MASC. 90-100 sum total as % of total corpus (includes exceptions to the MASC. 90-100's m. rules): 16,436/31,943 = 51.45%

FEM. 90-100 f.'s as % of total corpus (% of nouns in rule-conformity to FEM. 90-100's f. rules): 6,510/31,943 = 20.38%
FEM. 90-100 sum total as % of total corpus (includes exceptions to the FEM. 90-100 f. rules): 6,778/31,943 = 21.22%

% of m. and f. nouns in rule-conformity to MASC. and FEM. 90-100 rules (does not include exceptions to those rules):
15,853
6,510
22,363/31,943 = 70.01%

% of m. and f. nouns in rule-conformity to MASC. and FEM. 90-100 rules and to L rules (does not include exceptions to those rules):
22,363
2,598
24,961/31,943 = 78.14%

% of nouns covered by MASC. and FEM. 90-100 rules (includes exceptions to those rules):
16,436
6,778
23,214/31,943 = 72.67%

% of nouns covered by MASC. and FEM. 90-100 rules and by L rules (includes exceptions to those rules):
23,214
3,142
26,356/31,943 = 82.51%

APPENDIX E

NOUNS ENDING IN MUTE -e. (Graphemic categorization only.)

(I) Masculine 90-100%

	m.	f.	total:
-me(s)*	90.14 (1024)	9.86 (112)	1,136
-{b,c,d,f,h,p,r,t,ou}+ère	92.63 (88)	7.37 (7)	95
-{a,e,i}ste	97.07 (563)	2.93 (17)	580
-ge(s)*	94.15 (1368)	5.85 (85)	1,453
-dj			

(Nearly all nouns in this category end in -ge.)

(Note: not included as separate categories are the two nouns—both f. (*lieue, banlieue*)—which end in -*eue*, or the more numerous -*aie* nouns—58—which are likewise all feminine. Also not included are the 9 nouns, all f., that end in -*iée* or -*llée*.)

	m.	f.	total:
	93.23 (3,043)	6.77 (221)	3,264

---

*Very few nouns end in -*s* in categories where mute, word-final -*s* is listed as a possibility.

(II) Feminine 90-100%

	f.	m.	total:
-ade	90.64 (213)	9.36 (22)	235
-ude(s)*			
-elle	92.69 (203)	7.31 (16)	219
-ine	96.65 (433)	3.35 (15)	448
-ière	95.14 (235)	4.86 (12)	247
-${s \brace z}$e	90.03 (551)	9.97 (61)	612
-ie(s)* -ye	98.47 (1,736)	1.53 (27)	1,763

(Nearly all nouns in this category end in -ie.)

-ue(s)*	98.11 (52)	1.89 (1)	53
-oue(s)*	84.21 (16)	15.79 (3)	19

(See p. 5 of the ALPHABETIZED LIST for an explanation as to the presence of this category among the 90-100% overwhelmingly feminine.)

(Note: not included here as a separate category are the 35 nouns — 33 f., 2 m. — that end in -tée. These are grouped with the considerably larger category of nouns most of which end in -té. See p. 6, ALPHABETIZED LIST.)

f.	m.	total:
95.63 (3,439)	4.37 (157)	3,596

SUM TOTALS FOR MASCULINE 90-100% (I) and FEMININE 90-100% (II):

Total nouns in categories (I) and (II): 6,860

Masculine nouns in MASC. 90-100 as % of 6,860: 44.36%

Feminine nouns in FEM. 90-100 as % of 6,860: 50.13%

Total % of mute -e nouns covered by MASC. and FEM. 90-100 rules: 94.49%

Total % of mute -e nouns *not* covered by MASC. and FEM. 90-100 rules: 5.51%

---

*very few nouns end in -s in categories where mute, word-final -s is listed as a possibility.

(III) L(ARGELY) (70-89.9%) and M(OOT) (below 70%) in descending order (89.9% ⇒ 50.01%) by gender predominance:

(a) L f. predominants (6 categories):

	f.	m.	totals:
-ure	88.42 (435)	11.58 (57)	492
-V + ille(s)*	85.00 (238)	15.00 (42)	280
-s^c_x e	84.59 (829)	15.41 (151)	980
-oie(s)* -oye	76.19 (16)	23.81 (5)	21
ALL C + ère not b/c/d/f/h/p/r/t/ou:	74.07 (80)	23.93 (28)	108
-che(s)	73.54 (189)	26.46 (68)	257
	83.58 (1,787)	16.42 (351)	2,138

(b) L m. predominants (3 categories):

	f.	m.	totals:
-C + re(s)*	18.56 (95)	81.44 (417)	512
-aire	18.84 (68)	81.16 (293)	361
-fe(s)* -phe(s)*	22.90 (30)	77.10 (101)	131
	19.22 (193)	80.78 (811)	1,004

TOTAL NUMBER OF MUTE -e L's: 3,142

---

*Very few nouns end in -s in categories where mute, word-final -s is listed as a possibility.

(c) M f. predominants (6 categories):

	f.	m.	totals:
-t⎰t⎱e(s)* ⎩h⎭	69.15 (1,085)	30.85 (484)	1,569
⎧a⎫ ≠⎨e⎬ste ⎩i⎭			
-v(e(s))*	68.53 (98)	31.47 (45)	143

(Note: only 4 of the 143 nouns in this category end in -v or -s; the remainder end in -ve.)

	f.	m.	totals:
-gne(s)*	60.87 (42)	39.13 (27)	69
-pe(s)*	58.47 (107)	41.53 (76)	183
-ne(s)* ≠-ine	54.56 (341)	45.44 (284)	625
-de(s)* ≠-ade, -ude(s)	52.66 (228)	47.34 (205)	433
	62.91 (1,901)	37.09 (1,121)	3,022

(d) M m. predominants (5 categories):

	f.	m.	totals:
-be(s)*	40.37 (44)	59.63 (65)	109
⎧are⎫ ⎪Cire⎪ ⎪oire⎪ -⎨ore⎬ ⎪rre⎪ ⎪aure⎪ ⎩eure⎭	41.14 (144)	58.86 (206)	350
et al. (see ALPHABETICAL LIST, p. 2)			
-gue(s)*	42.47 (62)	57.53 (84)	146
-que(s)	45.30 (276)	54.70 (333)	609
-(l)le(s)* ≠elle	49.50 (449)	50.50 (458)	907
	45.97 (975)	54.03 (1,146)	2,121

TOTAL NUMBER OF MUTE -e M's: 5,143

---

*Very few nouns end in -s in categories where mute, word-final -s is listed as a possibility.

SUM TOTALS FOR L (III a., b.) and M (III c., d.):
Total nouns in III: 8,285
Total L's: 3,142
   Total L's as % of 8,285: 37.92%
Total M's: 5,143
   Total M's as % of 8,285: 62.08%

'LARGELY' TOTALS:
  L f.-predominant f. nouns as % of 8,285: 21.57%

                                                        = 31.36%

  L m.-predominant m. nouns as % of 8,285: 9.79%

'MOOT' TOTALS:
  M. f.-predominant f. nouns as % of 8,285: 22.95%

                                                        = 36.78%

  M. m.-predominant m. nouns as % of 8,285: 13.83%

GRAND TOTALS FOR ALL MUTE -e NOUNS:
Total mute -e nouns in corpus (6,860 (I, II) + 8,285 (III): 15,145
Cat. I nouns (overwhelmingly m.) as % of total mute -e nouns:
                        3,264/15,145 = 21.55%
Cat. II nouns (overwhelmingly f.) as % of total mute -e nouns:
                        3,596/15,145 = 23.74%
Cat. I and II nouns as % of total mute -e nouns: 45.26%
Cat. I and II nouns and cat. III L nouns as % of total
  mute -e nouns (6,860 + 3,142 = 10,002/15,145):   66.04%
Cat. III M nouns as % of total mute   = 100.00%
  -e nouns   (5,142/15,145): 33.96%
Mute -e nouns as % of total nouns
  in French (15,145/31,943):   47.41%
Total non-mute -e nouns in French: 16,798   = 100.00%
Non-mute -e nouns as % of total nouns
  in French (16,798/31,943):   52.59%
Mute -e nouns that are masculine: 6,629. (As % of total 15,145: 43.77%.)
Mute -e nouns that are feminine: 8,516. (As % of total 15,145: 56.23%.)

www.ingramcontent.com/pod-product-compliance
Lightning Source LLC
Chambersburg PA
CBHW051103230426
43667CB00013B/2420